DELIVERANCE
FROM
FAT
& EATING DISORDERS

by
BILL BANKS

Scripture Quotations are from the Authorized King James
Version, unless otherwise noted.

ISBN 0-89228-032-8

Foreword

I first became acquainted with Bill Banks and his ministry of offering Salvation, Healing, Baptism of the Holy Spirit and Deliverance in September of 1986.

I am a Doctor of Pharmacy (Pharm. D.) and so it was perhaps fitting that I should accept the Lord as my personal Saviour in connection with a medical/surgical procedure. I was diagnosed as having cholelithiasis (gall bladder disease) in March of 1986. I was allowed to personally observe the ultrasound which outlined my stones. I was then hospitalized for surgical removal of my gall bladder in September. When my surgeon told me he was unable to find any stones during my surgery, I asked, "How can that be possible?"

He answered by asking if anyone had been praying for me either before or during my surgery. I looked up to heaven and said, "Oh, my God, Yes!" I knew that my fiancee (now my wife) had had the prayer group she'd begun attending in Kirkwood lifting me up in prayer. The surgeon then described several other miracles which he had observed in the past few months. That day my life completely changed.

When I was released from the hospital, I went with my fiancee to the Thursday evening meeting in Kirkwood and met Bill Banks and his wife, Sue, for the first time. I walked into a meeting of 75 to 100 people who did not know me but loved me in a special way. As the praise and worship portion of the meeting progressed, the singing sent chills up my spine, and I knew I had found a spiritual home.

As an active health professional, I am continually amazed at the marvelous and magnificent love that God our Father has for us. He has brought patients to me in my clinical pharmacy practice in a general medicine clinic, that have been divinely healed or delivered from numerous non-curable ailments. (Non-curable by medical science but absolutely curable by the supreme and sovereign power of our God!)

The ailments which I have personally seen healed include (1.) a hemorrhaging peptic ulcer, (2.) scleroderma, a variant of rheumatoid arthritis that can only be managed and symptomatically treated with systemic steroids, (3.) oat-cell lung cancer eliminated within three months of diagnosis in my 81 year old mother-in-law, (4.) bilateral lung cancer (both right and left lungs) in a 55 year old woman, (5.) cardiomyopathy (damaged heart muscle) in a 60 year old woman, (6.) hearing loss in a 58 year old woman, (7.) my own healing from allergic rhinitis or hay fever. This is just a partial list of the healings that I have witnessed in the exciting past 18 months. Our God is so good, I can only assume that He continues to have people sent to me through the Holy Spirit, that have had remarkable medical experiences because of my clinical pharmacy practice.

I have also observed divine deliverance from manic-depressive illness, major depression, tobacco addiction, suicidal tendencies, insecurity, self-condemnation, self-persecution, indecision, unforgiveness and a variety of other conditions through Bill Banks and the Thursday night ministry. I firmly believe that the Lord has been doing a mighty work through the author of this book. I have personally been delivered from spirits of reincarnation, unworthiness, self-condemnation, driving too hard for unattainable goals, a phobia of flying in airplanes, fear of failure, compulsive eating, fear of condemnation, fear of disapproval, inferiority self-criticism and unforgiveness.

Clearly it is God the Father who is the Healer and Deliverer, and He has apparently chosen Bill Banks as one of His vessels for these blessings. Needless to say, I strongly recommend this book and its author to all who have a need.

Frederic Pfeiffer,
B.S., M.S., Pharm. D.

Table of Contents

PART ONE

Why Do People Overeat?

CASE 1 MARY'S STORY:
A FIRST ENCOUNTER WITH THE *SPIRIT OF*
THE FEAR OF STARVATION

Teaching Section I:
The Decision Element In Weight Loss

A. WHY DO *YOU* OVEREAT?
B. SOURCES OF WEIGHT PROBLEMS A-Z
   1. Poverty Syndrome
   2. False Poverty Syndrome
   3. Post Great Depression Syndrome
   4. "Clean Your Plate" Syndrome

Author's Introduction

Around the world countless people are spending millions of dollars on various methods and systems for losing weight. I venture to state that probably less than 1% of all those people have any true idea as to *why* they overeat.

I can sympathize with them for I have been engaged in a will-power battle on the 'weight front' for years. As a heavy teenager, I attempted to cover the embarrassment over my weight by joking about it. I used the old vaudeville line, "We fat people have to be jolly: we can't fight and we can't run." Of course, all fat people are not always jolly.

I have never yet met a heavy person who was even happy about being fat. On balance, it is important to recognize that some individuals may be satisfied being overweight, and, if so, that is fine for them. But for those reading this book, I feel it is safe to assume that you are among those who are unhappy about your present condition and seeking to overcome your weight problem. on.

Often when approached by someone in a prayer line, or in a service desiring to be delivered of an excess weight problem, I respond with the humorous old line, "I've got some good news and some bad news for you. The bad news first: This kind cometh not out but by prayer and fasting. The good news is — *that they do come out!*"

The Lord has revealed a number of unusual spiritual roots which cause overeating problems and disorders.

The following case which was first presented in *Songs of Deliverance,* is repeated here because it has ministered to hundreds of people and because it illustrates a significant and powerful truth about unnatural weight gain. (Weight gain is sometimes not at all natural. Some people may eat far less than others and gain weight, others may eat very heavily and not gain at all. Still others eat as a result of compulsions that they do not understand that have nothing to do with normal hunger or appetite.) This case presents an amazing account of an unsuspected source of an unnatural eating problem. . . .

CASE 1   MARY'S STORY

A FIRST ENCOUNTER WITH THE *SPIRIT OF THE FEAR OF STARVATION*

One evening a young minister came for deliverance accompanied by his wife. After he'd received deliverance, his wife said almost sheepishly, "Mr. Banks, I feel that I need some deliverance too."

I asked my standard question, "Mary, what makes you think that you have a demon?"

"I need deliverance from a *spirit of Gluttony*."

"You've got to be kidding," I exclaimed taken by surprise. But it was a natural reaction, Mary was what I would describe as being on the thin side of normal.

She then explained, "I know I'm not heavy now and don't look like it, but it's true, Mr. Banks. I am fine until spring rolls around, and I begin to think about getting into a swimming suit. You see I work as a secretary to supplement Jim's income, and I put weight on around my thighs. I am fine until spring rolls around," she repeated, "and then I begin thinking about putting on a swimming suit. The moment I make the decision to diet to take off the unwanted weight, *something in me just goes nuts!* I will go to the refrigerator and eat everything in it. I will eat until I become physically sick." Mary slumped back into her chair, tears filling her eyes. "I really want help," she said plaintively.

As she was speaking, the Lord revealed to me, perhaps

4

through a gift of knowledge, (I don't know how to explain it, other than suddenly I knew) that her problem was a *spirit of the Fear of Starvation* which she'd had from infancy! I asked, "What do you know about the early part of your life?"

Mary seemed a little startled but then smiled, and said, "It's funny you should ask, because the only thing I know is that my mother told me recently I cried for the first two weeks I was alive."

"Why did you cry for those two weeks?" I inquired following up on what I felt sure was a leading from the Lord.

"Because at the end of those two weeks the doctors discovered that my mother had an insufficient milk supply. They then gave me a supplemental bottle of formula, and from that time on I was fine," Mary explained.

Sometime during those two weeks, she had picked up the spirit of *the Fear of Starvation*. It never bothered her, never manifested itself, until she cut off the food supply. When the food supply was jeopardized, this 'thing' in her went berserk just as it did in her as an infant, and she ate everything she could get her hands on.

Mary was born-again, Spirit-baptized Christian prior to the time when she came for help. Shortly afterward she and her husband left the St. Louis area to minister in the northern United States.

OBSERVATIONS:

1.) Although Mary was a Spirit-filled Christian, her life was still influenced by a spirit which she had picked up in infancy.

2.) Her eating habits were being influenced by a force other than a naturally functioning appetite, or need for food. Her eating was compulsive! And it wasn't rational, because she ate without understanding why she was being compelled to eat.

3.) Mary's account gives an excellent introduction to abnormal eating situations where the source of the problem is supernatural.

4.)   If an evil spirit in a young Christian girl, the wife of a minister, can cause an aberrational eating pattern, from earliest childhood, then perhaps the same or similar sources could cause other eating disorders. I have found this to be exactly so; this book has been produced to attempt to offer aid to those who have battled long and hard with unnatural eating habits, or unnatural weight-gain. The other truths which will be presented, I trust, will be equally enlightening, and helpful.

5.)   Since this first encounter with this spirit, I've seen scores of cases of people whose problems were likewise rooted in the *Fear of Starvation*.

TEACHING SECTION I:

The Decision Element in Weight Loss

THE DECISION ELEMENT IN WEIGHT LOSS

All progress in the spiritual dimension results from a decision or a series of decisions made by the individual. Likewise the decision to be free is one that no one else can make for you. It is an individual decision of monumental proportion: it will affect both you and your offspring, perhaps for generations to come. It is a decision to obey God and enjoy life, health and prosperity, or to disobey God, reject His offered blessings and to have in their place death.

> "I call heaven and earth to record this day against you, that I have set before you life and death, blessing and cursing: therefore choose life, that both thou and thy seed may live: That thou mayest love the Lord thy God, and that thou mayest obey his voice, and that thou mayest cleave unto him: for he is thy life, and the length of thy days: that thou mayest dwell in the land which the Lord sware unto thy fathers, to Abraham, Isaac, and to Jacob, to give them:" (Deut. 30:19,20)

God has called heaven and earth to record that His royal proclamation might be witnessed by all the heavenly host, all the supernatural beings and by man. Satan was put on notice, as well as man, that mankind has a choice!

Most religious people and their structures refuse to believe this and have established elaborate means for man to somehow 'earn' a relationship with God by performing religious rituals, and for attaining acceptability within *their* structures by acting in certain acceptable ways, or by appearing pious. They and their organizations expect to be considered indispensable in mediating a relationship with God.

We have, nonetheless, been given freedom to think for ourselves. God gave suggestions and recommendations as well as commandments and statutes, His goal being to bless mankind and to prevent us bringing problems upon ourselves. I believe that probably seventy-five per cent of the people to whom I've ministered over the past seventeen years have had problems stemming directly or indirectly from someone disregarding and disobeying God's instructions concerning marriage.

The implied subject in the passage quoted above is you. The choice is yours, and no one else's. God will not make it for you. That would be fatalism, and would revoke His gift to you of free will.

This decision is unavoidable; to not decide is to decide. This is a spiritual truth: in Salvation, for example, to not choose Jesus and His offer of life eternal is to choose spiritual death.

In like fashion deliverance begins with a decision: a decision to put one's trust totally in God, to resist the enemy despite all his blustering attempts to instill fear, and to "call upon the name of the Lord."

God has done His part, He has done all, His work is finished. Jesus's work is complete. For another soul to be saved, He doesn't need to shed another drop of blood. From the cross He said "It is finished!" He meant it. (The Greek literal sense is "It is perfectly perfect and completely complete.") Nothing remains undone on God's part. His work is truly finished!

Thus obviously, the work that remains to be done is on our part. We must choose to accept or reject the gifts offered to us. It is just like the situation with a birthday gift: we have but two choices, to either receive or reject the gift. So it is with the gift of salvation, and with the gift of the Spirit. There is absolutely nothing we can do to make ourselves eligible. They are gifts freely given by means of grace, through faith, lest any man should boast.

God has designed man to think, to reason, and to exercise free will in order that he might be able to choose.

I have observed, and am certainly not alone in this observation, that one's religious persuasion or denominational background affects the way one deals with his frustrations and problems. The Baptists and Pentecostals, for example, take a strong stand against alcohol, while the Episcopalians do not. When the Episcopalian has a problem he is more prone to turn to the Martini tray to vent his frustrations, whereas the Pentecostal is more apt to go to the pastry tray, or cookie jar.

Thus we can see that the Pentecostals and Baptists who have exercised great restraint and resistance against alcohol, often may exercise little or none against food. Society tends to side with the Pentecostals condemning overindulgence in alcohol as unacceptable behavior, but attaches no stigma to overindulgence in food (gluttony); none at least, until obesity is manifested. However, the word of God makes no such distinction; it denounces gluttony and equates it with stubbornness, rebellion and with drunkenness. Scripture also expresses God's rather harsh view of the glutton, one who does not exercise self control in his eating habits.

> "And they shall say unto the elders of his city, This our son is stubborn and rebellious, he will not obey our voice; he is a glutton, and a drunkard." (Deut. 21:20)

> "For the drunkard and the glutton shall come to poverty: and drowsiness shall clothe a man with rags." (Prov. 23:21)

God certainly places the glutton in undesirable company, and it is awesome to consider how seriously God regards the status of the glutton. Sin is sin to God.

IMPORTANCE OF THE DECISION ELEMENT IN HEALING, DELIVERANCE, OR WEIGHT CONTROL.

"Do You Want To Cease Being Fat?"

In John 5:6 Jesus asked the impotent man at the pool of Bethesda, "Wilt thou be made whole?" A seemingly fool-

10

ish question, but it is true that not all people who have a need or a problem want to be free of their problem. When Jesus asks the question, "Wilt thou?" He is really asking of him, "Will *you* — do you wish to be, that is: will you make the decision to be?"

As you have probably gathered by now, there is a decision which you must make regarding your weight. Just as the alcoholic must come to the point of recognizing and admitting that he is an alcoholic before he can receive real lasting help, so must the glutton. Deliverance from any form of unnatural weight gain, or other type of demonic problem, requires the candidate to recognize that he has a problem, be willing to identify it by name, the same name by which he'd identify it in his neighbor, and then he is truly in a position to receive the deliverance he needs.

These decisions presuppose, of course, that the candidate is in a right relationship with God, the Deliverer, in a proper son-Father relationship with God and has met the other qualifications. (See *Songs of Deliverance*, page 116.)

WHY DO YOU OVEREAT?

We have discovered in more than seventeen years of counselling troubled people, that often to merely discover the specific name of the enemy has been the key to victory. In light of this truth, I offer you the following list of possible causes of overeating. Although this list is fairly extensive, it will not be all-inclusive. There are probably as many specific causes of overeating as there are people. However, it is very likely that you will be able to pinpoint your specific area of difficulty as you peruse this list.

There is a tremendous power in identifying the enemy. This is a lesson we learned in World War II; our servicemen were required to learn to recognize enemy aircraft by the shape, engine configuration, size and so forth. It is essential to be able to distinguish between friend and foe, ally and enemy. If we do not, we aren't receptive to aid from sources that would give it, and we aren't on guard against those we should. To know, for example, that the reason you overeat is due to habit, rather than a genetic condition, may give one sufficient faith to be able to gain the victory over the eating problem.

This is our sincere prayer:

"Lord Jesus, let each one who reads this material have the eyes of his (her) heart opened, supernaturally by You, to the truth that You would have him (her) to see, that he (she) might be set completely free to be all that you intended him (her) to be. Let every bondage to foods, or any unnatural weight gain problem be broken." Amen. As you pray this prayer with us insert your own name where appropriate.

POSSIBLE CAUSES OF OVEREATING:

Why do people overeat? Aside from the normal functioning of the appetite, causing one to eat when hungry, one may also eat as a matter of

SELF-GRATIFICATION

    A. *hunger*, indulging natural or unnatural appetites

Certain people are born with bigger frames, or larger bone structure than others, and may require more food intake. However, I strongly reject the fatalistic belief that one has to remain overweight, believing it to be totally true that with God all things are possible.

    B. To reward themselves (see Reward Syndrome)
    C. To sample something new

GLUTTONY

    D. A glutton is defined by Webster as "one inclined to eat too much, greedily; the act or habit of eating too much. One who does not exercise self-restraint or self-control in eating."

EMOTIONAL UPSET:
   I. **INSECURITY**
      E. Because of nerves or nervousness
      F. To escape an otherwise unpleasant reality. Exchanging a momentarily pleasant reality for an unpleasant one.

  II. **REJECTION**
      G. One may eat to alleviate the pain or hurt of rejection on one front. Hunger is fairly easily assuaged, and we can make ourselves feel good in at least one area by eating.

 III. **FRUSTRATION**
      H. Indifference: "I don't care anymore."
      I. Boredom
      J. "I give up on dieting," or "I can't get ahead at my job."

  IV. **AGGRESSION**
      K. Rebellion

   V. **ANGER**
      1. AT SELF
      L. Self-destruction

Strange as it seems, we have discovered that some overweight individuals with heart conditions who have been warned by their doctors that they are killing themselves by overeating keep right on overeating. They are literally killing themselves and are eating consciously or subconsciously to destroy themselves. In light of what has been learned in connection with the problems of bulimia and especially anorexia nervosa, this shouldn't surprise us. There often is also an element of "if I get sick enough he (they) will notice me, pay attention to me, or be concerned about me."

      M. Self-hate, often combined with rebellion. One young girl who came with *Self-Hatred* had been told by her father when he divorced her mother, "It's because you're so ugly." Thus she hated

13

herself, her appearance, and had no incentive to keep her weight under control.

    2. AT OTHERS

  N. Retaliation, that is to get even

An example of retaliation is the wife whose husband betrays her who either consciously or subconsciously retaliates against him by eating too much, perhaps because she knows he doesn't like *"fat women."* Her motivation may also include elements of self-reward, "I don't care" or self-destruction. (See case 9.)

VI. **FEARS**

  O. Being starved, or having at some point had an experience with starvation, causing a fear of starvation

  P. The fear that the food won't be there later; may include fear, hoarding food, or greed

ADDICTIONS

  Q. Addiction to almost any foodstuffs, popcorn, chocolate, cake, etc.

PHYSICAL CONDITIONS

  R. Physical problems, tapeworms, other natural health problems.

  S. Medication, can often affect one's appetite: the taking of drugs, whether legal or illegal, can also affect one's appetite.

  T. Alcohol or cigarettes, addiction to either of these (or drugs) can affect one's consumption of food.

An indirect example would be the beer drinker who begins to get a beer-belly, accepts his new shape and gives up on trying to stay in shape. He chooses his addiction over his appearance.

SEEMINGLY LAUDABLE MOTIVES

I. FRUGALITY
U. Avoiding waste, the fear of waste

Many people eat out of a fear (see Fears above) that the food may not be there later. In some cases this may have a logical root, as with those raised in orphanages or similarly strict homes where if the food wasn't consumed when presented, it was removed and nothing more would be available until the next meal.

POVERTY SYNDROME

Children raised in poverty or near poverty situations, often pick up a fear of starvation and a fear of not having enough of anything. This may lead to hoarding, or eating voraciously when the opportunity presents itself, and often functions as an incentive to do anything to avoid being in a poverty situation in later life. Many of the "Horatio Alger" stories of today are individuals who were raised in poverty, and seem to be compelled to succeed in order to avoid poverty. The fear of poverty is a strong incentive toward success for many people and for others toward problems in their lives. Uncontrolled eating and overweight conditions are common among those who have come from backgrounds of poverty.

FALSE POVERTY SYNDROME

An unusual variation which has also been encountered is that of False Poverty. There have been cases where the individual as a child somehow became convinced that the parents were poor, even though they were not, and he or she lived mentally as a child in danger of starving. The poverty was not real, a meal was never missed, but a *Spirit of Fear* had entered to convince the child that poverty and starvation were imminent. The fear may have entered as a result of being teased by a playmate who accused his family of being poor, overhearing a parental argument about finances, or an equally innocent remark made in jest such as, ''I guess we won't have enough money left to buy food this month.'' The result for the susceptible child, however, is just the same as if it *had been fact*; because he believed it to be the truth. Children often have difficulty differentiating between reality and fantasy, between fact and fiction.

However, a far more widespread root is to be found in the after-effects of the Great Depression.

POST GREAT DEPRESSION SYNDROME

Many of us who were raised as 'post-depression' kids, were raised by parents who had been confronted with the specter of people out of work, poverty, facing the actual possibility of starvation. It affected them with a fear which was often transmitted consciously, sub-consciously, or demonically to their children. Similarly children who were raised in homes which experienced poverty, who frequently missed meals, or were forced to eat very substandard or unnourishing food, often picked up eating disorders, or compulsions.

Very frequently eating disorders may have more than one root, or may be reinforced in a variety of ways. The following syndrome is a clear example of how overlapping pressures are exerted and with the corresponding guilt over the weight gain, gives an example of the whipsawing effect of the contrasting pressures.

THE ''CLEAN YOUR PLATE'' SYNDROME
HUMANITARIAN REINFORCEMENT

Another unusual factor commonly involved in cases of overeating is the ''clean your plate'' syndrome. When my generation was growing up we were told to clean our plates because of the poor starving people in India, or Africa. No one ever explained how my eating the last few spoonfuls of spinach or carrots was going to prevent the starvation of an African or Indian, but the guilt trip was nonetheless laid upon us. To this day, I still have to make a conscious decision of my will, in order to be able to leave any scrap of food on my plate.

A few years ago I suddenly realized that I was eating everything on my plate whether I wanted it or not, out of habit. I used to beg my wife to put the food in serving bowls on the table, rather than on my plate. If she put the food on my plate, regardless of whether I was hungry or not, I'd eat whatever was there. If she put one pork chop on my plate, I'd eat it and be satisfied. If she put three pork chops on my plate, I'd eat them: if two chicken breasts, I'd eat two. I suddenly came to realize that I had neither the sense nor the will power to put the food back on a serving platter or leave it. I ate whatever I found on my plate. There had been a habit instilled, a guilt trip deeply entrenched that somehow I was helping the poor and the starving, by cleaning my plate.

RELIGIOUS REINFORCEMENT

This was reinforced by a religious aspect of the problem. During my youth, and perhaps still today in some areas, there was a gimmick employed to help American children identify with mission programs. Our church participated in a "sacrificial meal program" in which we either passed up a meal, or ate typically meager fare such as would be eaten in India, or some other foreign country. We would eat for example one bowl of rice, and the cost of what we would have otherwise eaten was then collected by the church to be sent to a particular mission.

PATRIOTIC REINFORCEMENT

The fetish for cleaning the plate was further reinforced by the World War II era, and the Victory Gardens. These were gardens in which everyone who was able was encouraged to plant vegetables and attempt to help raise food, because the government was experiencing food shortages and instituted 'rationing' of existing food supplies. The very fact that there were shortages, and fear manifested by our parents with regard to the food supply, created fear in many that food would somehow not be there later; so eat what you can, while you can, and don't waste any scrap of food. This naturally also laid the ground work for more over indulgence. Thus all these laudable, frugal, humanitarian, religious, and patriotic pressures helped cause the "clean your plate" syndrome to become deeply entrenched within many of us.

SOCIAL PRESSURES, OR CUSTOMS

V. Social Courtesy: It's someone's birthday and out of consideration for their feelings you eat a piece of cake when offered one, even though you aren't at all hungry.

TIP

There is a familiar old quote concerning orange juice, that

"It's gold in the morning,
Silver at noon, and
Lead at night."

This old adage, I believe, also holds true with regard to other food stuffs. If one can change one's eating patterns, one can lose weight without even dieting. It has always seemed to me that if we could reverse our eating habits, instead of eating our largest meal at night, and generally smallest meal in the morning, as social custom dictates, it would be beneficial. If we could reverse that arrangement, it would be much easier to control our weight. We need the food and the energy more in the morning after the longest fast time in our day, and we need them the least prior

18

to going to bed for the night.

Surprisingly, this simple theory which struck me in childhood has been confirmed through recent research. A study at the Department of Nutrition at Tulane University School of Public Health, (as reported in *Muscle and Fitness Magazine*, 2110 Erwin Street, Woodlands Hills, CA 91367) has shown that overweight people "who eat a heavy breakfast, a light lunch, and an afternoon snack, but no food for the last eight and one- half hours they are awake, can lose five to ten pounds per month." Science has confirmed what I've known logically from my youth. For more tips on controlling your weight, see the Weight Control Tip Section at the end of this book.

The Bible states that the truth can set us free. Simply recognizing the truth about why we overeat, can be sufficient to break a gluttonous hold over us.

As mentioned, we often eat too much food at night when the calories are not going to be consumed. It's very easy to rationalize eating large meals at night for social reasons. At our home, my wife has rationalized eating big meals at night, "because we need to have the dinner meal with our boys." Our boys being healthy teens involved in sports and athletics, do have huge appetites by dinnertime, even though we don't. She has promised repeatedly, "When the boys go off to college, we'll eat less and have smaller meals at night." She has made good on her promise since our youngest has entered Wheaton as a freshman.

People often find themselves eating, not out of hunger, but

> *to please* someone else
> or, *to not displease* someone else.

W. Actual coercion.

The husband of a new bride finds he must eat with relish whatever she prepares or she'll cry. Later she may become a pushy wife, who says, "You don't love me if you don't eat what I have fixed." Coercion usually works in combination with some of the other categories.

A reverse aspect of coercion is that of the person who was forced to eat something distasteful to him as a child and who in later life is unable to eat that type of food. The child who throws a tantrum and refuses to eat beets, and is subsequently forced to eat them, perhaps accompanied by much apparent anger upon the part of the parents, may be unable to understand why as an adult he has in addition to the dislike of their taste, such a strong emotional reaction when served beets.

X. Habit, Custom, or Family Pattern

Traditions, customs, and family gatherings often center around meals. If everyone around you is eating huge meals, it's difficult for you not to do likewise. If you go to any inexpensive smorgasbord, the all-you-can-eat type restaurant, you'll usually see families who have overeaten to the point of becoming grossly overweight. Mother is overweight, and therefore regularly prepares too much food, and the children are encouraged, or allowed to over indulge. It is a medically established fact, that fat cells in endomorphs and therefore tendencies toward overeating are established very early in life, usually in the first few years of life.

A loving wife can be of great assistance to a husband or child who is seeking to control weight, and a wise wife can also help herself in dieting by not buying or keeping in the pantry the kinds of high calorie snacks which might be great temptations, such as candy, peanuts, cookies, pies, cakes, etc. She can instead provide healthy low-calorie snacks. I am always amazed to see in the home of someone who claims to be seeking to lose weight, a five pound box of chocolates, or bowls of nuts.

BAD EATING HABITS

Bad eating habits are something familiar to all of us. Some are a result of early training, or lack of training in the home. Some result from undue indulgence of the child's eating whims. Other bad habits are a result of situations or circumstances that develop later in life. As an example, people who live with diabetics who must eat regularly, often eat frequently themselves, because of habit, custom, or environment, not hunger.

Y. Pride: pride in eating a lot, in being a "big-eater"

A subtle motivation to over-eating may be the desire to hear once again, "Good girl, you've cleaned your plate." Pride is often instilled in the child with praise for eating more than usual, for being a "big-eater."

Many times children and teenagers are complimented and "bragged upon" by parents and adults, as well as their peers for their ability to consume great quantities of food. Sometimes the adults merely express their pleasure by laughing at their eating habits, or quantities consumed. But the effect is nonetheless the same, the child realizes that he has created happiness, pleased his parents or attained some degree of positive status by eating a lot. Everyone seems to have had parents, grandparents, or other loving relatives who "loved to see youngsters eat," and encouraged them to "eat their fill."

Many teenagers with weight problems, who carry them into adulthood, can trace the root to a pride in how much they could eat. I recall relating to my parents when I returned from a grade school trip by train to our state capital, the quantity of food I'd consumed: three candy bars, several sandwiches, and then at the capital, a chicken fried steak dinner with mashed potatoes, cole slaw, dessert, and then three sandwiches on the return trip. On another occasion at a 4th of July function with unlimited soda available, I drank seventeen bottles of soda. It was almost a game to see who could consume the most. The end result, was as you might expect, an undisciplined appetite, with which I battled for years.

Recognize an important point. No evil intentions were

involved on the part of any of the individuals who helped reinforce my eating habits. They all were loving, kind, moral people making statements that were all natural and normal, yet contributing to an undisciplined appetite, and a tendency toward gluttony.

FATALISM

Z. Inheritance

If one believes he or she is going to be overweight because "it's in the genes," there will be no faith to resist the tendency to overeat.

Such thinking erodes faith and the desire to change. It attacks, or destroys motivation to diet; to exercise self control, and leads to the "I can't change, I'll always be this way" mentality.

1. Self-Fulfilling Curses

The child or young person who is unkindly called unflattering names by playmates, parents, siblings or other relatives, may find it difficult to overcome that designation. Especially hard to handle are those nicknames applied to the child by loved ones. Dozens if not hundreds of people have passed through our prayer room who have testified to the pain, hurt and anguish which they have suffered as a result of being called by their unthinking relatives, "Fatso," "Blimp," "Fatty," "Whale," "You're Fat," "You're Plump," "You're pleasingly Plump." The net effect of such nicknames on the individual is all too often to accept and believe them, and to thus adopt the rationale "if my loved ones view me this way, then everyone else must also. My parents who love me, say I'm fat, I must be fat!" The result is a lack of incentive to be thin.

2. It's God's Will

"God made me this way, He must want me to remain fat." "God created me with this weakness for ____ (you can substitute here any appetite you know that you over-indulge, or for that matter any other tendency toward sin — shoplifting, sexual immorality, cursing, smoking, drinking, etc.), and therefore He understands, and accepts this behavior." God certainly does understand the behavior, but He doesn't excuse it. He expects us to exercise both our will power, and what is probably the least popular fruit of the Spirit, Self-control!

Note that the Scripture uses the word "self-control" rather than "God-control." Man is responsible for his own decisions, and has free will with which to make them. Man also has a responsibility to ask God for help when needed, in order to be able to truly say, "I can do all things through Christ which strengtheneth me." (Phil. 4:13)

Clearly the decision is yours. Probably ninety percent of those who read this book can be helped by the truths contained thus far. The ten percent who haven't found their answers here should seek deliverance.

Do only children or infants such as Mary, pick up spirits of the *Fear of Starvation,* or is it possible for adults to also get them? The next case answers that question. . . .

PART TWO

Fear of Starvation Can Also Be Acquired in Adulthood

CASE 2   FRANCIS TAKESH CASE

Teaching Section II:
Appetites and Their Functions

A friend of mine often states, "Many people are killing themselves with their forks."

Fear of Starvation Can Also Be Acquired in Adulthood

The fear of starvation does not merely enter in infancy, as it did with Mary; it can also come during adulthood, at any time there is sufficient trauma or fear, as the following case illustrates.

CASE 2   FRANCIS TAKESH'S STORY

Ten years ago, Francis, a woman who had been married to a Moslem called for an appointment, primarily seeking deliverance from a *spirit of Gluttony*.

When she arrived she explained, "I married Abdul, or Abe as we called him, while we were attending college out East. Abe had been raised a Moslem, but appeared to have been completely westernized."

She had divorced him about ten years previously, but still had problems forgiving him for the hurts which he had caused her. The deepest hurts were ingrained as a result of his mistreatment of their children. She had been deeply wounded when he told her he really didn't care anything about the children and had only had them out of curiosity "to see what they'd look like."

It is very difficult for those of us in the western world to grasp how differently the Mohammedan mind views things and how really cruel they can be. They are not influenced by Christian morality, can be terribly cruel and think nothing of it. Their attitude toward women's roles and their treatment of women are totally unthinkable to us.

She explained that everything seemed fine while they lived in this country, his "westernization" appeared to be complete. However, about four years into the marriage he received a phone call from his family telling him to return to Tehran. He promised her that everything would be wonderful there, too. He would get her a new house, a car and they would live well.

"Almost as soon as we arrived there, he reverted to the Moslem way of life," she said sadly. "Although I didn't have to wear a veil, we lived as Moslems. The promised house didn't materialize, we lived with more than twenty of his relatives in one two-room house. He began treating me the way the other men treated their women, beating me physically. But the verbal abuse was worse for me than the physical. He totally destroyed my self-worth. I arrived home with no self-esteem whatsoever. I truly thought that I was as 'worthless a piece of human flesh' as he'd been telling me that I was. While over there, I not only feared for my life and the lives of my children, but I was afraid that I'd never be released from Iran. In fact, I couldn't have left if he hadn't changed his mind at the last moment and signed the papers permitting us to leave."

"The men seemed to eat adequately, but there was never enough food left for the women and children. I really believe I was starving." Then Francis blushed and tears of shame filled her eyes, "I stole scraps of bread and ate them in the middle of the night when the hunger pangs awakened me."

"In fact," again she blushed, "I still have those hunger pains in the night, and I either have to take food to bed with me, or get up and go down to the kitchen and eat." She continued, "This has to be demonic, I hate it! There is no reason for me to be hungry in the night, and I often don't even remember eating until I find the dishes the next morning."

"I have forgiven him repeatedly [indicating that it hadn't been effectual], and I have prayed and prayed against this weight problem and the eating thing, but all to no avail!"

I then explained a little to her about the way demons operate, how devious they can be, and how they try to con-

vince us that the troublesome manifestation is of our nature, and not theirs; that she was 'just that way,' greedy
and dominated by her appetite. I related to her the story
of Mary's *Fear of Starvation*, explaining how subtle demons
can be. I then led her in a prayer to forgive her ex-husband
for all his cruelty to her and to her children, for his rejecting them, abusing them, ignoring them, and for other
wrongs not pertinent to our discussion here. Then we commanded the *spirits of Rejection, Hatred, Fear, and the Fear of
Dying in Captivity in a Foreign Country* to leave in Jesus' name.
Finally we commanded both the *spirit of the Fear of Starvation,* and the *spirit of Starvation* itself to leave as well.

Francis later called to tell me that although she felt she
was delivered totally, that she still had a problem: she would
sleep walk and eat in her sleep without waking up at all.
We prayed together and commanded both the *Sleep-Walking
Spirit* and the *Subconscious Spirit of the Fear of Starvation* to
leave her.

Francis's testimony today is that she is free of these tormenting spirits and is beginning to lose the unwanted
weight.

OBSERVATIONS:

(A.) She, like so many others assumed since there was
an appetite and weight problem, that what she was up
against was *Gluttony.*

(B.) As a Christian, she knew she should forgive but
hadn't received adequate teaching on the mechanics of ac-
complishing forgiveness. (See the teaching section on Forgiveness in Vol. 1, *Songs Of Deliverance,* pp. 79-87)

(C.) Trauma, fear, disillusionment and deprivation
opened her up to the invasion of the evil spirits. In the same
way veterans who have been P.O.W.'s or have otherwise
suffered deprivation of food, have picked up the same type
of spirits.

DELIVERANCE TECHNIQUES EMPLOYED:

(1.)   Listening carefully to her account, we were able to pinpoint when the trouble with her weight began (upon returning to the United States) and what preceded it.

(2.)   We were able to share the forgiveness teaching with her and lead her through the steps to forgiveness, eliminating one basis for the demonic influences to remain.

(3.)   We were also able to share with her the account of Mary's problem with the *Fear of Starvation*, giving her a basis for understanding her own manifestations, and a foundation of truth upon which she could stand to resist the enemy.

REVELATION:
A SPIRIT OF THE *FEAR OF STARVATION* CAN ALSO ENTER AN ADULT IN A TIME OF TRAUMA.

REVELATION:
A SPIRIT CAN MANIFEST ITSELF WHILE THE INDIVIDUAL IS ASLEEP, OR SLEEPING.

Francis's problem as we discovered was more than a mere matter of appetite. . . .

TEACHING SECTION II:

Appetites and Their Functions

APPETITES AND THEIR FUNCTIONS

APPETITES:

Appetites are something normal, natural, and God-given, intended by our Creator to keep us healthy, able to function fully as His children. However, when Satan is able to get hold of an appetite, he takes that which is good and normal, intended for our good, and twists, and perverts it, causing it to work against our good, and even uses it as an instrument of torment against us.

Eating and drinking are normal activities, but when Satan gets involved with an appetite it goes berserk: it can cause us to eat too much (gluttony) or not enough (starvation), or too much of the wrong thing (addictions, or compulsions, such as for sweets, alcohol, drugs, or food fetishes and fear-motivated fixations, such as to be healthy one must drink carrot juice, cranberry juice, eat protein, or health foods). Balance is needed along with common sense!

One delivered from alcoholism isn't delivered from all drinking, merely from the problem liquid, alcohol; just so, the person delivered from cigarettes doesn't quit breathing in air altogether, merely from inhaling poisonous cigarette smoke. In like manner, the person delivered from gluttony is often only delivered from the addictive substance be it chocolate, desserts, sweets, junk food, snacks or from the unnatural aspects of his eating habits.

A demon of gluttony merely utilizes an appetite which Satan has perverted and distorted so as to make it a problem. God designed man with certain natural appetites which are part of His creation and are therefore obviously good in themselves. But when Satan through some snare is able to distort and pervert that normal appetite into something abnormal, then it becomes a problem. Some of the more hideous and bizarre addictions are usually inflicted only after some serious contact with the occult and are mentioned here only by way of illustration. We have encountered cases of people addicted to drinking their own urine and behaving in other socially unthinkable ways and yet none of them was beyond the Lord's ability to help. Don't forget the essential, exciting truth, "nothing is too difficult for the Lord" and if He was willing and desirous of freeing, and bringing peace to, these poor, troubled souls . . . then He can, without a doubt, help you if you sincerely desire to be helped.

When Satan becomes involved, he perverts, and distorts, causes the normal to become abnormal, aberrational, out of balance, twisted or warped. Bulimia is just such a work of his, and several of his devious methods will be exposed in the case of Barbara whom we shall meet shortly.

PART THREE

Recognized Eating Disorders: Anorexia Nervosa

CASE 3 GIGI JONES
CASE 4 SUZANNE

Teaching Section III:
Exercise Profiteth Little

*Make Jesus Lord of your **fork** and **knife**,*
*as well as the Lord of your **life**.*

Anorexia Nervosa

Anorexia Nervosa is defined by Webster as a "personality disorder, chiefly among young women, characterized by aversion to food, obsession with weight loss, etc." It is often first treated as a medical problem, and then usually referred to the psychiatric department. Some notable cases have been recorded as responding to the latter treatment, and sincere Christians have given great praise and credit for their healings to the psychiatrists and their methods. However, we have seen this horrible disease from a different vantage point and have been led to treat it as a spiritually rooted problem. We have seen deliverances occur, setting women totally free, when the demonic spiritual roots are cut.

Our first case will give an introduction to the way God led us to deal with this disease. . . .

CASE 3   GIGI JONES

"I know you . . . help . . . er . . . pray for people." John was clearly uncomfortable and struggling for words. Although he ran a business a few doors from our Christian bookstore, we'd only met once or twice. "The daughter of the lady in the shop next door to mine is in serious trouble. The doctors say this 15 year old girl is dying. They can't figure out why, and they can't help her. She just either can't or won't eat. She's starving. I just saw her and she only weighs about ninety pounds. Could you try to help her?" he asked, obviously relieved to have finished his task.

"Sure, John. Just send her down," I replied somewhat surprised to learn that a positive report must have circulated about our very quiet, almost under-cover, backroom prayer room operation at the bookstore. It hadn't occurred to me that any of the business people in the neighborhood were even aware of our ministry efforts, even though the Lord had been doing mighty and exciting things there for several years at that time.[1]

A few minutes later John returned with her, introduced us and excused himself. As soon as Gigi entered our store, I knew she must be the one. The sweetest little emaciated face was smiling at me from atop a body that looked as if it had just been released from Dachau. "Hi, I'm Gigi Jones," she said in a weak, little girl's voice that seemed bubbly, but somehow tinged with sadness.

As we walked to the prayer room I was again struck by how very thin she was. Her little arms and legs seemed to have no meat on them at all. I began to experience the old anger for Satan welling up within me for what he'd done to this poor child and a Godly love for her was beginning to grow. (I can report to you that the love is still there ten years later.)

Gigi began her story, "As you can see, I'm skinny." She giggled and then her voice became serious. "I weigh only 89 pounds, as of the last time I weighed. I haven't weighed in about a week because I'm sure I've lost more weight and I don't want to worry my mother any more than I already have. I've been to all kinds of specialists, and the best they can come up with is that perhaps I have a new disease they're calling anorexia nervosa. It apparently hits primarily teenage girls, and basically means that the victim is, for some reason, involuntarily starving herself to death. Several girls have already died of it, and they are starting to study it, but very little is really known about it so far. The only clue they seem to have is that usually the girls hate their fathers. But *I* don't! I don't want to die either, but I don't know how I can help myself."

---

[1]Some of these accounts are recorded in the other books by the same author, available in the back of this book.

I asked, "How long have you had this problem?"

She thought for a moment and replied, "I guess a little over three years, but it has really only gotten serious recently, about the last three to six months. It's awfully silly but I think of myself, or I did until recently as fat. I used to eat and then make myself throw up, so I wouldn't gain weight." Gigi blushed slightly, as she continued, "But I haven't done that for three weeks now." She said, brightening again, "Now I do realize that I have a problem and I do want to get well."

Gigi was a sweet little girl. There was something almost childlike about her, and in a certain way she seemed much younger than her physical age. Her father had divorced her mother about four years before, leaving her with inner hurts and scars. Gigi had three sisters, and a brother, none of whom had any evident eating problems.

I suddenly realized that there was another and more basic problem, "Gigi, are you saved?"

"I don't know what you mean. I belong to the big Presbyterian Church my family has attended for years. I have gone to the Sunday school and youth groups and we often have good times, but I don't think that is what you mean. Is that being saved?"

"Not quite." I said as gently as I could, "Being saved is having a personal relationship with Jesus Christ, being 'born again' into a new life, and being assured of heaven. Do you know, for example, where you'd be right now if you'd been killed in a car wreck this morning?"

"I would *hope* in heaven, but I really don't know," she replied openly and with complete honesty.

I then explained Salvation to her, how she could be saved and born again. When given the opportunity, Gigi eagerly accepted Jesus as her Lord and Saviour[2] and also received His peace.

Recognizing that Gigi was going to need all the power

---

[2]See the advertisement in the back of this book for the tape HOW TO BE SAVED, OR BORN AGAIN!

she could possibly obtain from the Lord to overcome the spiritual enemy that was seeking to destroy her life, I then asked, "Have you ever heard of the Baptism of the Holy Spirit?"

"No I haven't. What is that?"

I gave her my explanation of the Baptism. She then said, "I believe I need that too." So we prayed for her and she entered into a new relationship with the Lord. She seemed to be starving for the word of God and received it hungrily, just as her physical body was starving from a lack of natural food.

We had now spent several hours, getting her story out, explaining Salvation and the Baptism, and answering her other questions. Since she needed to get home for her afternoon rest, I suggested, "We've probably covered enough for one session. I don't want to tire you, but I do want to pray for your healing before you leave." So we prayed for her to be healed of her condition, and I bound the *spirit of Anorexia Nervosa,* knowing that the spirit and I knew what was happening even if Gigi didn't yet understand spiritual warfare. Having extracted from her a promise to try to eat that evening and to return the next day for another session, she left but first gave me a big hug. A deep God-given trust and love was growing between us.

In our next session, I explained to Gigi about demons and how they operate, and that I was certain that her problem was neither natural nor physical, but was rather a demon called *Anorexia Nervosa.* This spirit I explained to her, was operating in her much like a spirit of *Self-Hate, Self-Destruction,* or conventional *Suicide.* It was just using, instead of poison, a gun or carbon monoxide, *Self-Induced Starvation* as a means to take her life.

"How do I get rid of these things?" Gigi asked totally open to whatever new truth or ministry God had in store for her.

I explained the steps: "The first step is
1. to recognize the spirits as real, to identify the real

enemy,

    2.   to determine to make a decision to break with him, to refuse him a place (''give the devil no place''),

    3.   to renounce him,

    4.   to turn to Jesus, prayerfully as Deliverer,

    5.   to call upon Him and His power to set you free,

    6.   and to cast out the spirit; command each one whom you recognize within yourself to leave you in Jesus' name.''

Gigi obediently went through the steps and finally commanded each spirit to leave her in Jesus' name. She was so pathetically weak and frail, God lovingly granted her a very gentle deliverance. She was so thin and fragile a quick movement might have broken a bone. Gigi said afterwards, ''I really do feel better. I feel as if something has happened, although I'm not sure just what. I'll trust that Jesus is healing me.''

After each of our sessions Gigi found that she was better able to cope with her problem. She began regaining strength after receiving the Baptism in the Holy Spirit and her first deliverance.

In the next session, I introduced the subject of forgiveness and encouraged her to forgive all those whom she felt had wronged her. I especially encouraged her to

    forgive her father   for divorcing her mother,
                        for hurting the family,
                        for hurting her mother,
                        for hurting her sisters and
                        for causing her embarrassment, and shame

    forgive her mother   for her part in the divorce,
                        for blaming the father,
                        for not being able to meet all her needs

When Gigi had forgiven her parents and everyone else who had treated her unkindly including those who had mocked her because of her condition, we then cut all ties with *Unforgiveness* and the *Root of Bitterness*. She also admitted at this time that she was aware that she didn't really want to grow up. She would have preferred to remain a little child. With very little grasp of the whys involved, we prayed against this hindrance to her healing, and cast out the spirit *that really Didn't Want to Grow Up*. We have since come to discover that this is a very common spirit among children of divorced parents, especially girls, who seem to cease growing or maturing emotionally at the point of the divorce. Perhaps this is in reaction to the trauma of it, or probably more likely, it is an attempt to blank out the whole painful situation. We learned more about this spirit that "didn't want to grow up" and its nature very shortly in connection with "Little" Barbara and her bulimia.

Anorexia Nervosa seems to strike girls without a good relationship with an earthly father, or who never experienced unconditional love from an earthly father. Missing love, or feeling unloved, unwanted, unaccepted, sets the stage for a spirit of the *Fear of Abandonment*, which is far stronger than a mere spirit of rejection. The spirit of *Abandonment* is an extremely strong root fear, for it is really a fear of death, itself. The rationale goes something like this, "if my father, or mother, or parents, don't love me, then they may give me up, put me in an orphanage, or merely *leave me* or *abandon me* . . . and without food, clothing and shelter, I will die." This spirit of *Abandonment*, I believe will be often, if not always, found to be present in cases of Anorexia, and probably also in *Bulimia*.

* * * * *

I really hurt for those who have missed the blessing of a loving earthly father. I was blessed with such a father, and a wonderful mother as well, and decided as a child that when I grew up I wanted to be a good father to my children. However, the greatest gift that a father can give his children is to love their mother, provide for them a stable home, and to love them unconditionally. Children, to be emotionally healthy, need to know the love of their parents. An Old Testament practice which we have allowed to lapse, which should be reinstituted, is the custom of the father pronouncing a blessing upon his children.

The blessing, spoken in the presence of the child, could be as simple as a prayer to the effect: "You are my child. I love you and I am proud of you." It could be more extensive. A prayer and a blessing which I have pronounced upon each of my two sons, may serve as an example:

"You are my son. I love you and I pray that you will have a long and happy life, find challenging work that you enjoy, marry a good Christian girl who will be a good and faithful wife, and have children which will bless you as you have blessed me."

* * * * *

Our goal in ministry is to attempt to cut all the roots which may give Satan any legal basis for attacking, to remove any basis the demons may have for attaching themselves to an individual. In the natural we know that flies are drawn to dead or rotting flesh. In a spiritual sense our goal is to eliminate the rotten flesh within the individual: to eliminate taints of sin which attract Satan's flies. That's why we instructed Gigi to forgive those whom she knew or thought had wronged her; we were eliminating the enemy's claim upon her because of unforgiveness or the root of bitterness, which had been allowed to spring up.

Gigi returned several months later to report that she was now able to eat (although she had to consciously resist the problem for a season), was able to return to school full time, and was back at her straight "A" level. One spring day about six months later Gigi came bubbling in to tell me that she'd been accepted at a college on the East coast which had offered her a full four year scholarship. She planned to study pre-med with a goal of going into psychiatry in order to be able to help others with eating disorders. I rejoiced for her, although I inwardly felt sure that she was on the wrong track: she was pursuing the wrong avenue of approach. It wasn't medicine or doctors who had healed her, but the power of the Living God and the ministry of His deliverance that had set her free.

Gigi has now completed her four years of undergraduate school, her pre-med course and finished her graduate work. Since switching from her original major, she is now engaged in medical research working with eating disorder cases. According to her last letter she still loves both her work and the Christian fellowship group which she has been attending since moving to the East coast community.

OBSERVATIONS:

1. Gigi's openness before God and receptivity for all that He had available for her made her an excellent candidate for deliverance and healing.

2. Her lack of an earthly father's love had contributed to her problem. Young girls often may not receive the desired and needed love of a father because the father is alcoholic, is divorced from her mother, or perhaps because he is deceased. A common pattern seen in these cases is that such a young girl often tries to be perfect in order to win the approval of other men, so that they will love her. This is especially true of girls who have lost a father through death or divorce. Another common but very different pattern is that some will often become wild or promiscuous looking for the love they so desperately need. We have ministered to dozens of women who had to marry early because they were unwise in their searching for the love missing from their lives due to the absence of a father.

DELIVERANCE TECHNIQUES EMPLOYED:

1. As a fairly classic case, Gigi received first our number one message: Jesus as Saviour. Then she met Him as "He who baptizes with the Holy Spirit" and received from

Him the power which He had promised in Acts 1:8.

2.   We took things more slowly than I would have preferred, due to the frailty of her health. We ministered to her only as she was able to accept in each session, endeavoring not to overburden her, and to be sensitive to her physical weakness.

3.   Forgiveness was an important key to her healing and deliverance.

REVELATION:
ANOREXIA NERVOSA WAS CLEARLY A DEMON IN THIS CASE.

REVELATION:
ANOREXIA NERVOSA WAS ACTUALLY A SPIRIT OF SUICIDE, SELF-HATE, OR SELF-DESTRUCTION WHICH MANIFESTED AS *SUICIDE BY STARVATION.*

Gigi was to be only the first case of deliverance from *Anorexia Nervosa,* for apparently word of her healing became known. . . .

CASE 4   SUZANNE'S STORY

Another lovely young girl came for prayer, confessing her need to be set free from *Anorexia Nervosa* after hearing of Gigi's victory. She, too, received Salvation, as did her entire family, and was later Baptized in the Holy Spirit, along with six other members of her family. We prayed deliverance for her from the spirit, and she, too, was set free.

The eating disorder block was removed, within a few months she met the "right" young man and is now married and raising a family. Often young women who have eating disorders, either anorexia nervosa, or bulimia, seem to fear marriage because "my husband would find out about it and reject me," or because "I would just be so ashamed."

TEACHING SECTION III:

Exercise Profiteth Little

EXERCISE PROFITETH LITTLE

Many of the young women in the early stages of eating disorder problems will attempt to include exercise as a means of obtaining thinness. As their disorders progress they usually become too weak to continue with an exercise program.

Exercise can help in weight control to some degree, but the Scripture is apparently correct when it says, "for bodily exercise profiteth little" (I Tim. 4:8). Diet and obesity experts agree that one has to walk more miles, run more miles, or strenuously exercise for more time than is practicable to have much effect upon weight, unless there is a significant change in eating habits.

To lose weight one does need to make the decision not to do push-ups but to do "push-aways," that is "push-aways" from the table. You must push *yourself* away from the table. The table won't push away from you, and the Lord won't push you away from the table.

"Debbi Diet"

(1.)   A fairly common aspect of weight fetishes in this country today is what we might designate as the "Debbi Diet" Type: one who has become a follower of one of the various health and fitness gurus, enticed by the allure of becoming a "perfect woman" by virtue of eating right (usually minimally), dieting and consistent exercise.

(2.)   The typical individuals in this category are the young divorced women who crave approval, acceptance, and re-establishment of their self-worth. There may often be additional motivating factors:

(a.)   to attempt to win back their husbands,

(b.)   to prove themselves attractive, persons of value and worth,

(c.)   to prove to their children that their father was crazy to have left, (d.)   to retaliate against the ex-husbands by being so attractive, so shapely, so trim, so non-undesirable, that no one could believe anyone in his right mind would divorce her. This is also a striving, in essence, to prove that they are not fat, not overweight, not-unattractive, or any of the normal reasons for being rejected.

"Little" Barbara's case beautifully illustrates the fear women develop that some loved one will discover their secret weight problem, especially bulimia, as we shall see in the next case. . . .

PART FOUR

Recognized Eating Disorders: Bulimia

Teaching Section IV:
Motivation — Key to Success

"If you're putting on weight in the wrong places, stay out of those places."

There are certain places we know we shouldn't go, if watching our weight, certain restaurants such as smorgasbords, for example, or those that specialize in desserts. If we're having trouble resisting desserts, that's the kind of place we should avoid.

Bulimia

Bulimia is defined by Webster as "a continuous abnormal hunger." Bulimia like anorexia nervosa is usually treated initially by dieticians and the medical profession, who often turn the cases over to psychiatrists, and now more frequently seem to be referring patients to eating disorder clinics which offer a combination of these various medical specialties.

We, however, attack this problem from a spiritual viewpoint and have discovered, not surprisingly that like anorexia, bulimia responds to deliverance, once the spiritual roots are discovered and cut.

The first case took several years to obtain the victory, but the battle was well worth it for the Lord revealed many things to us through "Little" Barbara. . . .

CASE 5   "LITTLE" BARBARA'S BULIMIA

A sweet young woman rather small of stature whom I'd known for several years as a customer of our store, asked me for an appointment. I had prayed with her on several occasions in the past for the healing of relatives, and had had a number of discussions with her over the years about the Baptism of the Holy Spirit. So her request didn't surprise me, but her opening statement did.

"Mr. Banks, I need help. I have a problem with *Gluttony.* My Baptist church doesn't believe in demons or deliverance, but I know that this thing is a demon. I have fought it and fought it, but it still compels me to eat . . . even when I'm not really hungry . . . and more than I want or need. I hate it. And . . ." she continued

51

quickly as if fearing she'd lose her nerve, "it's worse than just plain gluttony. I make myself throw up after I go on one of these eating binges so that I won't get fat." She blushed with shame, and I realized how severely this thing had been tormenting her.

"Do you think you can help me?" she asked intently.

I shared with her that I knew the Lord desired her to be free of the bulimia condition even more than she wanted to be free, and that I knew He would give her the victory if she'd keep seeking Him. "But let me ask you a few questions first. Are you saved?"

"Yes, I definitely am," she said firmly. I asked a few probing questions to be certain and, satisfied that she was, I continued, "Have you been Baptized in the Holy Spirit?"

"Well, that depends on how you define the Baptism in the Holy Spirit," she waffled.

I explained the Baptism in the Spirit fully to her[1] and then asked if she'd like to receive. She said she'd have to think it over, because it was foreign to her church's teaching and Barbara then asked, "but can we pray for my condition now anyway?"

I shared honestly with her that I felt she needed the Baptism, that she needed all the power that God had available for her if she was to get and maintain freedom from the demonic power which had established such a grip on her, but that we would certainly pray. I prayed for her healing and took authority over the *spirit of Bulimia* binding it, and commanded it to leave.

I feel that the individual needs to come to a position of calling upon the Lord, *themselves*. They can't always rely upon someone else's prayers. So, I normally have each candidate for deliverance take authority and command the spirits to leave, themselves.

In the weeks that followed she reported several times

[1] An explanation of the Baptism of the Holy Spirit and how to receive it is to be found in *Alive Again!* by the same author, and available from Impact Books, Inc.

that she could tell a difference and was much improved.

Nearly a year later, "Little" Barbara again made an appointment and came to the prayer room. "Mr. Banks, although I'm greatly improved, this bulimia is still with me. I want to get married but I really don't feel I can as long as this has hold of me. It wouldn't be fair to my husband. I don't even want Paul to know about this."

"Are you ready for the Baptism?" I asked teasingly; I had been gently nudging her about it for several years, and had in our previous session told her that I felt she needed it.

"Yes, I think I'm finally ready for the Baptism." She responded with conviction.

So once again I explained the Baptism to her, and then prayed with her to receive, which she did. She had a sweet release in a heavenly language.

"Now," I said, "we're ready to get this job done."[2]

Once again we went delving for the roots of this spirit of Bulimia. Something was different now, there was a new power at work. "When did this thing first seem to be a problem, or when did you first begin to feel that you were eating too much?" I inquired.

"I really haven't any idea. It seems like it's always been with me at least from my earliest teen years."

As we prayed and asked the Lord to help us find the key, she suddenly remembered something. "It doesn't seem to have any bearing, but I just remembered *not wanting my breasts to grow.* I guess I wanted to keep on being 'my Daddy's little girl.' I guess I didn't want to grow up."

Suddenly everything began falling into place. I realized now why everyone had always thought of "Little" Barbara as "that cute, little Barbara," and why when she spoke in that soft little whispery voice, there seemed to be an almost childlike quality about it. She always seemed depen-

[2]The Baptism in the Holy Spirit is not necessarily a prerequisite for either healing or deliverance, but it can certainly help. It is also an indication of a willingness to yield to and obey the Lord rather than one's own mind.

dent, somewhat gullible, and naive, even though she had been very successful in a rather worldly career.

It was clear now. She hadn't wanted to grow up; had made a decision, a choice, to 'remain a little girl' and in the process perhaps had verbalized this wish as "I hate my breasts," or "my fat" or "I pray I will never put on weight." Somehow an invitation had been extended to, or an opening been made for this *spirit of Bulimia* to enter.

Praise God! We now had a clue and a handle on this spirit. We could now cast it out and close the door through which it had entered behind it. After "Little" Barbara had commanded *Bulimia* to leave her, I took over.

"You *demon of Bulimia,* I command you to leave Barbara now. Come out of her in Jesus's name, and you spirit that entered her when she made that decision to 'not grow up,' you *'Little-Girl spirit'* come out." She gagged a few times, jerked, and was free. "I think it's gone!" she said with her face breaking into a big grin.

Six months later, just before her marriage, Barbara stopped by to thank me again, and tell me that she'd not had any recurrence of the problem, nor any self-induced regurgitation since her deliverance. She's now happily married and raising a family. Again, the significant fact to be noted is that the bulimia responded to deliverance!

OBSERVATIONS:

(1.) Although "Little" Barbara had the desire to be free, she apparently also required the additional incentive of love for someone else to motivate her to seek God for deliverance wholeheartedly.

(2.) She *hated* the effect of the thing manifesting itself in her life. Such hatred of the demonic manifestation is usually a prerequisite for deliverance. Jesus has promised to deliver us from our *enemies,* but not from our *friends.* We have to come to the point of hating the demonic influence, like David, with a "perfect hatred."

54

(3.)   Clues to her root problem were visible, but uninterpretable without the sovereign revelation from the Lord.

(4.)   One can apparently invite a spirit or open the door for one by verbalizing dissatisfaction with the body, personality etc. that God has given. She had made an inward decision not to grow up.

DELIVERANCE TECHNIQUES EMPLOYED:

(1.)   Patience was required to await God's timing to bring "Little" Barbara to a point where she could trust Him for her deliverance. God allowed the "test of time" to prove to her the validity of our ministry. Several years lapsed between the first gentle witnessing to her of the healing power of God and the Baptism of the Spirit, before she actually sought prayer for her own condition.

(2.)   It is often helpful to determine when the evil spirit first began to manifest its presence in the candidate's life. Jesus seems to employ this technique in Mark 9:21. This often gives clues to the nature of the spirit and the method by which it gained entry, when compared with other circumstances or occurrences in the person's life.

An example of such a case was a woman who came to us who had been "bedridden, on and off, for eight years with undiagnosable sicknesses." The doctors acknowledged that the afflictions were real, but were unable to detect the source. Simply by probing for what had happened eight years previously, we discovered the source of the problem. She admitted to having committed adultery, and an unnatural sex act. The guilt and shame over her sin had literally made her sick. We had her confess the sin, renounce it, and command the spirits involved to leave her. We then prayed for her to be completely healed. She left rejoicing, and later reported that the Lord had indeed healed her completely.

(3.)   We asked the Lord to provide sovereignly for our lack of knowledge as to how to deliver "Little" Barbara, "having done all . . ." that we knew how to do, and determining ". . . to stand," trusting in Him. We stood still awaiting the deliverance of the Lord. He made up for our lack, giving the candidate the missing key.

REVELATION:
BULIMIA WAS A SPIRIT IN THIS CASE.

REVELATION:
EXPRESSING DISSATISFACTION WITH THE BODY, PERSONALITY, ETC. WHICH GOD HAS GIVEN CAN APPARENTLY GIVE AN OPENING FOR A DEMON.

REVELATION:
A KEY TO THIS DELIVERANCE WAS DISCOVERY OF THE *"LITTLE GIRL"* SPIRIT!

Although we were blessed 'beyond measure' by God's gracious deliverance of Barbara, the Lord had still more to teach us through Janet. . . .

CASE 6   JANET'S STORY

I received a tearful phone call, from a girl who identified herself as a friend of another girl who had recently received the Baptism at our store, and then told me that she had just finished reading our book *Ministering to Abortion's Aftermath,* and felt she needed some help. I invited her to come the next day to our prayer room.

She was a very lovely young girl of about 27. It became apparent that she was seeking, in part, the love and affection of a father that she'd never really experienced. We dealt with the issue of the abortion, which was confessed both as abortion and as murder; she repented and both corresponding spirits were commanded to leave. Janet experienced a fairly classic deliverance with tears flowing, and nose running.

Janet next admitted that she had another problem for which she needed help: she was both an alcoholic and bulimic. As Janet described her alcoholism, I was reminded of Old Pierre, an alcoholic cook, on a ranch where I had worked as a boy of 17. I soon learned that Old Pierre was known as a complete, hopeless alcoholic. He was a fabulous cook but had lost every good job he'd held as chef, even at the famed Waldorf Astoria Hotel in New York, because of his drinking. Some of the hands told me, "Old Pierre is nuts! He'll drink anything with alcohol in it, shaving lotion, cooking sherry, hair tonic. He'll strain some of it through bread to filter out the worst of the poisons."

I recall visiting Old Pierre once in the hospital. Unfortunately at that time I was only capable of extending help on the natural compassion level, and took him a carton of cigarettes. In those days I wouldn't have even thought of praying with him.

As I mentioned Old Pierre's case to Janet, she teared up with shame and said, "I'm the same way; I'll even drink Listerine."

On one occasion she had broken into a relative's home by removing a door, and once inside, unscrewed the door to the liquor cabinet and had gone on a six-day binge.

Janet was saved and baptized in the Spirit on her first visit to our prayer room. Then we prayed about the drinking problem. We cast out *Alcoholism,* but realized there were more spirits. In subsequent visits, we developed a good rapport, and friendship. She was lovely and sincere, but acknowledged that she was weak, and felt she was unable to resist the alcoholism and bulimia.

In the process of ministering to Janet, we uncovered more about the damaged relationship with her father. Her father as she described him was both an alcoholic and a worka-holic.

For a year or more the battle within Janet raged. She was fine for a while, and then went on a binge. It became longer and longer between binges, but she still was not completely free. Freedom from the alcoholism came first. She called and came to see me tearfully, remorsefully, totally self-condemned because of 'falling off the wagon' and going on a week or weekend drunk. Later she came with the same reactions to an eating binge that she had had at first with the drinking bouts. "How could Jesus still love me? How can I really be a Christian and drink like this? or defile my-self by all this eating?" Satan whipsawed her with the sin and then the condemnation. When she was drunk, Janet often went back to the young man she'd lived with pre-viously, although she had broken off with him after our first prayer session together.

I next received a call from Janet who said, "I'm locked up in a detoxification program here in St. Louis; could you come and visit me?" I went to see her and prayed with her, encouraging her to utilize whatever methods she felt led or had the faith to use.

Upon her release from the program, she came again to the prayer room and we dealt with the spirits of *Alcoholism* and *Bulimia*, praying in agreement and commanding them to leave her body. This time she seemed ready to trust the Lord for the deliverance.

I was quite shocked to receive a call from her a few days later telling me her parents had arranged for her to go to a second detoxification program out-of-town, because the first program had not worked. "By the way, those prayers we said about the Lord reversing the effects of the alco-holism upon my body really worked! I've been an alcoholic for ten years and bulimic for six. (Which includes inducing vomiting to rid my body of the effects of the binge eating.) And," she paused for a breath, in her excitement, "they told me they couldn't believe the tests they ran on me. My

58

organs are all perfect. Liver and kidneys are fine, no indication at all in my body chemistry that I've been leading this kind of life. God has either healed, or totally shielded me from the effects.''

I had a strong sense that the previous deliverance had been successful, and that she was already completely free, but didn't feel led to try to tell her what to do. Such a decision to stand on deliverance, or any promise of God's, must be made by the individual. She called me several times while out of town to tell me that she felt sure she was already delivered before she went. When she returned, she came to see me to report that she was free and felt the out-of-town program had been largely a waste of time for her.

About a month later I received another tearful call from Janet for an appointment. She came greatly disturbed, but with an apparent inner peace. She said, ''I don't know if you can forgive me, but I'm pregnant! I know I shouldn't have let it happen, but this time is different. I really believe what I read in your abortion book, and I wouldn't even think of having an abortion. I couldn't now as a Christian. I told Tom and he's asked me to marry him. What should I do? What's the Christian thing to do at this point?''

After a long and serious talk, she said, ''I really appreciate your help, I'm going to tell him, 'Yes.' ''

Janet called me from the hospital recovery room two hours after her baby girl was born. I visited the next evening with an ecstatic couple of young parents and rejoiced with them over the birth of their new baby.

A dozen years before ''Little'' Barbara came for help, I had first heard of bulimia from Roberta. . . .

CASE 7 ROBERTA

In 1973 or 1974 another woman came for help due to the symptoms of bulimia before it had apparently become a recognized problem. She was a very attractive young Christian mother who was deeply guilt-ridden over her eating problem. We prayed for her healing and deliverance, not really sure what the exact nature of the problem was. She experienced some immediate relief, but had to do battle with the habits involved for a season, during which time she came for prayer on several occasions. Various related problems were dealt with as they surfaced.

She moved from our immediate area, and I rarely saw her. However, I spoke with her again recently when she called with a prayer request, and I asked how she had been since her deliverance. She shared a few important insights. "I found I had problems with bulimia in times of frustration, or when I was having feelings of insecurity or lack of self worth. However, when I was strong in the Lord, I had no problems with it."

The love and acceptance of the Lord offset her feelings of fear, insecurity and frustration. Like Peter, when she was able to keep her eyes upon the Lord, she was fine. When she took her eyes off the Lord and looked to her own circumstances, focused upon her fears, she would fall back into her problem.

Today the medical and scientific communities have taken notice of this particular type of eating disorder and bulimia has become a familiar household word. Common symptoms of anorexia nervosa and bulimia are fixations upon food, seeming to be unable to think or talk about anything but food, dieting and being thin. Another observable symptom in severe cases is discolored teeth, which become gray due to the repeated contact with the stomach acids in regurgitated food.

Studies have shown that one-third of bulimics have had at least one parent who was alcoholic. This would plant the roots of rejection within the child, leaving the child feeling the need for love and acceptance. It also leaves the child insecure, and helps the enemy plant the roots of the *Fear of Abandonment*. Binge eaters are very similar to alcoholics; they overindulge. Other commonly attendant circumstances are depression, guilt, shame and thoughts of suicide.

God was preparing to refresh my memory and ministry by means of a revelation in regard to Minnie's bulimia. . . .

CASE 8   MINNIE

Minnie, an attractive young woman, slightly overweight, arrived at our prayer room with a fairly common story: she had grown up in a home with an alcoholic father, with whom she had no real relationship. The father was a carouser, flagrantly unfaithful to her mother. There was conflict in the home; she didn't feel loved. Her father was finally divorced by her mother, when Minnie was about fourteen. He remarried and that also caused her hurt. She was continually being forced to take sides between the two factions, alternately being pressured to side with her mother or with her father. When she was eighteen, her mother died; and her father died about three years later.

Minnie related a history of sexual sin and shame. Continually seeking love, acceptance and affection which had been denied her in her youth, she was guilt-ridden over her own repeated fornications. She also related having several abortions, and experiencing several of the classic abortion symptoms.[1] Minnie had at various times been quite confused and upset by the hatred which she felt for her own daughter.[2]

Minnie, wanting a normal life and being basically a good girl, tried marriage, but it broke up shortly as had all her various relationships. She got a divorce, and felt it to be only the culmination of a whole series of failed relationships. She became suicidal and had actually attempted to take her own life. A year or two after her divorce Minnie became a Christian and was baptized in the Holy Spirit.

Minnie, as noted, was a fairly classic case. In the preliminary interview it was determined that her weight prob-

[1]For additional information see *Ministering to Abortion's Aftermath.* (Available in back of book.)

[2]*Ibid.*

lem included *the Fear of Starvation,* and a *Fear of Being Fat.* The whipsawing fears caused her to become bulimic, eating and then forcing herself to regurgitate.

We shared with her the story of Mary with which she identified tremendously. When Minnie was born her mother had been ill with a chronic condition, which was discovered shortly after she was born and later diagnosed as muscular dystrophy. So that the milk supply was probably deficient, as well as insufficient.

Minnie confessed to a *Hatred of Men.* She had also experimented with *Witchcraft,* in an attempt to gain some control over her situation, and similarly dabbled in the *Occult.* She'd experimented with an *Ouija Board,* and subsequent to that time had been cursed with *Precognition,* (knowing in advance things that would happen).

There was apparently a curse of *Poverty* over the family, but it was only one of several. There was the curse of *Alcoholism* in her father's line. A curse of divorce was apparent in that her mother was *Divorced* and all six of Minnie's sisters were divorced. She herself had been divorced. All but one of her six sisters had already had *Abortions,* as had she. At least two or three of her sisters were married to *Abusers,* and one of the children in her family had been born as a Down's Syndrome child; and others had a variety of physical afflictions. "Everyone in my family," she said, "has always been *Unhappy,* and I have been cursed with *Bulimia* for years." Spirits of *Infirmity* were also rampant within the members of her family.

All the spirits mentioned thus far were commanded to leave and dealt with according to the procedures indicated in *Songs of Deliverance* and *Ministering to Abortion's Aftermath.* When the deliverance was over, mascara dripping from her chin, Minnie said, "Oh, I feel so much better."

We were just about to leave the prayer room when suddenly I remembered a spirit which I should have prayed against with her, but had overlooked in connection with her bulimia.

I said, "Minnie, there is another spirit that I feel we probably ought to deal with, and that's the "*Little Girl*" *spirit:* the *Little Girl spirit* that didn't want to grow up, that wanted to always remain 'Daddy's little girl.' "

She began to sob profusely, and cried out, "It's true, it's true! I never did want to grow up, I always wanted to be just a little girl. I just wanted to have somebody take care of me, to be somebody's little girl, to be loved, to crawl up in someone's lap and be protected and cared for."

My heart thrilled with gratitude to God for reminding me to come against the *Little Girl spirit* that is so often present in bulimia cases.

As beautiful as this experience was, God had in store for me a really strange case in Bobbi. . . .

CASE 9   BOBBI

An attractive, well-dressed, young, professional woman sat across from me in my prayer room visibly shaking.

"I'm terribly nervous, but I knew that I had to come and see you. I've had bulimia for fourteen years and it is ruining my life. I even have three sizes of clothing hanging in my closet at home, so that I can have something to wear when my weight fluctuates. I'm now afraid of losing my husband; I don't know how much longer he'll be able to put up with me."

She gulped for air and continued, "The Devil continually works me over. I eat and then he condemns me for having eaten; telling me if I were really a Christian, or a good Christian, I wouldn't fall prey to these bulimic temptations." Tears filled her eyes as she said, "I'm really desperate. I'm *Suicidal!* If I can't get some help I might as well end it all. As a Spirit-filled Christian, I know that's crazy. I mustn't end my life, but that's how I feel."

I discovered Bobbi hadn't read *Songs of Deliverance* and so I related Mary's story to her.

"Wow! That's exactly my case too. My mother breast-fed my three older brothers, but when I and my two sisters were born, she either didn't have sufficient milk, or the new thinking that bottles are better influenced her. I've been told they did have trouble, finding a milk that I could tolerate. My two sisters have the same problem I have with bulimia, although theirs isn't nearly as bad.''

Together we cast out the spirit of *Bulimia,* the *Fear of Starvation,* and the *''Little Girl'' spirit.* With each of them Bobbi had a violent reaction. We had joined our right hands to pray at the outset and her grip on my hand became so tight that my fingers turned blue. It was obvious that she was being set free, so I didn't mind. Shortly she loosed her grip on my hand and rocked back and forth, turned red in the face, coughed a few times and then said, ''Wow! I can't believe how much better I feel.''

Bobbi called a few days later to thank me and to relate that all was ''fabulous.''

Four months later I received another call from Bobbi who was in tears, desperate and in pleading tones she said, ''I've got to see you right away, my *Bulimia* has come back on me.''

When she arrived and was seated in the prayer room, she explained, ''It's back and it's worse than ever.''

I was surprised to say the least, and asked, ''How long were you free of the bulimia after the first deliverance?''

Her eyes lit up as she said, ''It was fabulous. I was truly free from the torment and fear of the bulimia for about four months. But then I had a dream. I dreamed about having bulimia and eating and the next day it was back and worse than before! What did I do wrong? How did I let the spirit of *Bulimia* back in?''

''I don't think you did anything wrong. I suspect you may have a different spirit that is manifesting, or perhaps even a second spirit of *Bulimia* that has surfaced.''

''That could be, I guess. This one is different and worse than the other one. This one is so bad, I've even been growling like an animal in my sleep. I've scared my poor husband half to death. He isn't a believer yet, but he told me I'd better call 'that Banks guy' who prayed for me before. So at least something positive is coming out of all this; he's coming to see that there is tremendous power vested in spirit-filled Christians. But I'm really desperate, and I'm feeling suicidal again.''

''Tell me about your dream,'' I asked hoping to find some clue.

''There wasn't much to this dream. I was just in a situation where a lot of food was available to me, and I began to eat even though I felt it was wrong as I was doing it. I realized as I began to eat that it was the old binge type of eating. In the real world absolutely nothing happened to trigger it. My job was fine, my home life was fine, and I was feeling better about myself than I had in fourteen years.''

''I think I should tell you this, actually I had two dreams. I had the first one shortly after I was here for prayer. In that dream I was with my mother and I saw something black and horrible on her back, like a big (she made a volley-ball sized gesture) black, spider or something equally hideous. I was terrified and called out to her, and then I realized as she turned to face me that the thing had somehow jumped over onto me. I woke up shrieking in fear and shaking.''

I responded, ''Well, it seems obvious in the earlier dream that something had been transferred from your mother to you. Has your mother had a problem with bulimia or weight problems?''

''Oh, no, not at all. She is a little heavy, stockily built, but she isn't concerned about her weight and I've never known her to diet. She is truly a fabulous cook and people love her food. She is generous and really loves to give food to people, cakes, cookies, and other dishes.''

''In fact, she has always pushed food on us kids. She doesn't seem happy or secure unless we are all eating a lot. She fixes big portions and really 'feasts' us when we go over for meals. When she comes to visit our house, she always goes immediately to the refrigerator and pantry to see that there is plenty of food in the house.''

''That seems a little strange, doesn't it?'' I asked gently, and as she nodded in agreement, I continued, ''Could your mother have a *Fear of Starvation* or a *Fear of Poverty*? Did she have enough food when she was growing up?''

''Of course,'' Bobbi exclaimed. ''That's it! She didn't have enough food. She was a child in Germany during World War II, and they never had enough food.'' She continued excitedly, ''She rarely ever talks about those days, but once I overheard her and her brothers talking about how they would go to the garbage dump to hunt for scraps of food to eat. They were at times at the point of starvation! So sure, she does have a fear of starvation and a fear of poverty, and that's why she is so concerned about everyone else having enough food to eat, and their pantries filled. I never realized it before, but she has always hoarded food at home. They always had more food than they really needed. Even though my parents are well-off financially and go shopping every weekend, she probably has a six-month's supply of food in her pantries and freezers.''

It was becoming clear that Bobbi's problem, which had been sovereignly revealed in the dream, wasn't her own *spirit of Bulimia* coming back, but her mother's *spirit of Bulimia* manifesting itself. She had inherited the spirit in the womb, or it had been subconsciously implanted, or taught to her in her formulative years.

This time I had Bobbi command ''the spirit of *Bulimia*, the *Fear of Starvation* and the *Fear of Poverty* which she had picked up from her mother'' to leave her. Once again there was a fairly violent manifestation with coughing and gagging, confirming to us both the validity of what we'd been shown concerning this *inherited spirit of Bulimia*. We also commanded *Suicide* to go in Jesus' name. Bobbi was again ecstatic. ''I felt them go! And I feel fabulous once again! I can't thank you enough for everything.''

I responded, ''Thank the Lord who revealed to you the

spirit, and who has by His power set you free. It's truly His ministry; He is the DELIVERER!''

OBSERVATIONS:

1.   All the classic spirits which we would have expected to find in conjunction with Bulimia were here: *Bulimia, Fear of Starvation,* and the *Little Girl Spirit,* plus the secondary inherited spirits of *Bulimia, Fear of Starvation,* and the *Fear of Poverty.*

DELIVERANCE TECHNIQUES EMPLOYED:

(1.)   Persistence was a key in this case. It was also necessary for the ones ministering not to become discouraged, nor to allow the Enemy to cause us to doubt God's power or desire to set this captive free!

REVELATION:
A SECOND SPIRIT OF *BULIMIA* WAS PRESENT, AND HAD BEEN INHERITED FROM THE CANDIDATE'S MOTHER.

God had more surprises awaiting us in ministry with an old friend, Charity, who suddenly turned up with bulimia. . . .

CASE 10   CHARITY

Charity, whose deliverance from a *spirit of Suicide* was told in *Songs of Deliverance,* called again for an appointment for deliverance fifteen years later. Although she had come several times over the years for various healing needs, this was the first time she had a real deliverance need. Satan fought her coming with a vengeance. Three different times the appointment was scheduled, and then she had to call to break it because one of her children became sick with the flu. Finally she called and said, "I'm coming for this appointment, no matter what!"

"I thought I was coming to see you mainly for a physical problem that I have. I think I have 'T.M.J.' (Tempro Mandibular Joint). I can't eat solid food without it causing me great pain, and right now I can't even eat meat because it is too painful." Charity swallowed hard and continued, "But I now realize that I've got an even bigger problem. I need to be delivered from a *spirit of Gluttony!*"

"I'm ashamed to even mention it but it is so unbelievable. I read your book on deliverance, *Songs of Deliverance* and I was especially touched by the "fear of starvation" case, although I definitely don't have that one."

She seemed so positive. I was led to ask, "Were you breast-fed?"

"No. My mother had heard that breast-feeding might cause the breasts to sag, so she elected not to breast-feed any of her kids."

Charity continued her account. "I can't believe how much food I eat. If I'm asked to bake a cake or pie for church, I make it and then I eat the whole thing myself. I then have to run to the store for more ingredients to make the one for church. I feel like such a hypocrite! I tell my kids not to eat junk food, and I do buy good healthy snacks for them: apples, celery, and that sort of thing, but secretly I buy myself a two pound box of chocolates and eat it alone. I feel like an old dog or animal hoarding his food."

"I fix myself a snack," she said hurriedly as if eager to get the story out. "And then eat dinner with my family. But while I'm cleaning up after, I eat all the leftovers and even eat the scraps off their plates."

"It's been awful, but what really convinced me that this thing was a real problem and demonic, was something that happened a few weeks ago. I was eating in secret and I started to choke on some food that lodged in my throat or windpipe, but I found myself still stuffing food into my mouth. Even while I was choking, *this thing* made me keep right on eating. I almost passed out before I dislodged the food and got a grip on myself. That's when I called you the first time for an appointment.''

Charity said, ''I've made up a list of the spirits as you suggested in your book, and here's what I think I need to be prayed for.''

As she read from her list I compiled my working copy:
1. Gluttony (compulsive eating)
    I added
2. + Fear of Starvation
3. Bulimia
    A. ''Binge'' Eating
    B. ''Sneak'' Eating (or eating in secret)
    I added
4. + the ''Little Girl'' Spirit
5. Selfishness
6. Spoiled   (She had been spoiled as a child: raised as an only child, and never had to learn to share.)
7. Inferiority (had always felt inadequate; not as bright or talented as others.)
8. Jezebel: she mentioned an eighth problem which illustrates how deviously Satan strives to prevent us losing weight and improving our self-image. ''I haven't been able to lose the weight that I gained after having my sixth child, and I think I know part of the reason. Several years ago I lost a *Jezebel Spirit* in a prayer meeting where your wife spoke. I've had the fear that if I were to lose the excess weight, I'd get the *Jezebel Spirit* back again.''

I explained briefly to Charity what spirits we'd be dealing with and how I suspected they'd entered. I then prayed, took authority over the spirits and led her in commanding the first spirit, *Gluttony*, to leave her in Jesus' name.

When I commanded the spirit of *the Fear of Starvation* to leave, the reaction was both violent and classic. She coughed, turned quite red in the face, and gagged several times. I smiled inwardly remembering how sure she had been that she "definitely didn't have that one."

Having completed my list of spirits, and sensing that she still wasn't completely free, I commanded any other spirits that were tormenting her to manifest themselves, to name themselves and to come out. I also instructed Charity that as soon as she heard a spirit name itself in her mind, or in her ear, to name it out loud and to command it to leave her in Jesus' name.

Immediately she responded, "*Self-Righteousness!*" I had her command that one to also leave her in Jesus' name, which she did, and again there was a violent reaction. The spirit first manifested itself as *Pride* sometimes does, by causing her to "puff up." She stretched to her full seated height, extended her chest, pulled her head back at a haughty angle and stuck her chin out.

I commanded *Self-Righteousness* to come out a couple of times and then she bent forward, gagged, coughed profusely and again snapped herself back up into the rigid upright position. But something then began causing her back to writhe. She groaned in pain and lifted first one shoulder and then the other, as someone might who was experiencing a muscle spasm in the back. Her upper back and neck seemed to be involved too. She began working her head from side to side and stretched her neck.

In addition to *Self-Righteousness*, seven other spirits named themselves and were in turn commanded to leave:

1. *Cowardice* (She identified it as "Cowardly," and so we used her terminology.)
2. *Lying*
3. *Insanity*
4. *Indecision*
5. *Procrastination*
6. *Self-Righteousness* (This was a second spirit of *Self-Righteousness*, the main focus or characteristic of which was "Fault-finding.")
7. *I'll Never Amount to Anything"*

Finally it was over, and she was free. She looked up and

said, "Wow! I'm free!" She asked only half-joking, "Do people ever die during these sessions?"

I agreed that she'd certainly had a rough, violent deliverance. Surprisingly far more violent than had been her deliverance from *Suicide*. (See Case #1: "Deliverance Defeats Suicide" in *Songs of Deliverance*.)

Charity called me the next day to say that the T.M.J. pain had completely left her, and that she was able to even eat steak. She was also able to eat any other kind of food; her jaw was completely healed.

OBSERVATIONS:

1.   Once again, the common mis-diagnosis of gluttony was applied because the main observable manifestation was a tendency to overeat.

2.   Note also Satan's subtlety in causing her to fear losing her weight, telling her that if she did, she would again get the *Jezebel Spirit*.

3.   In this case also, the presence of a spirit caused a physical manifestation and pain.

REVELATION:
A PHYSICAL CONDITION, T.M.J., WAS CAUSED IN THIS CASE, BY A SPIRIT OF *SELF-RIGHTEOUSNESS*.

TEACHING SECTION IV:

Motivation — Key to Success

MOTIVATION — KEY TO SUCCESS

In order to lose weight, there must be an incentive to diet: motivation is a key. Sometimes all one really needs, in order to be able to successfully diet, is sufficient motivation. Merely wanting for years to lose weight may not have offered a teenager sufficient incentive to get the job done. Yet, let that same teenaged girl suddenly become interested in a young man, and that which was formerly impossible becomes not only possible, but may seem almost easy.

Others who have never been able to discipline themselves have found that making a decision to have attractive, well-kept "temples" (I Cor. 3:16) for Jesus, has provided them the added incentive to get the job done. Still others, realizing that temperance or self-control is a fruit of the Spirit, determine to exercise it in the area of eating.

A key God has given us concerning gifts is that to use the gift honors Him, and tends to keep the gift flowing. As with guidance, if I refuse to obey the first thing God tells me to do, I wouldn't plan to hold my breath until I get the next word from Him. He expects us to obey and to use what He has given us. To not use a gift is to dishonor the Giver and is on a par with disobedience.

Unbeknownst to me, I was about to learn more about the *Spirit of Gluttony* and its roots. . . .

PART FIVE

Gluttony Rooted in Sin & Sin Roots of Eating Disorders

CASE 11 OLIVIA
CASE 12 EDITH: FEEDING HATE
CASE 13 JEANNE: REBELLION/REJECTION

Teaching Section V:
Skinny Gluttons / Fat Deliverance

*Candy lovers can appreciate a quotation from Shakespeare who said that "There is a **divinity** that shapes our ends." Divinity being a candy, it can indeed have an effect upon the **shape** of our bodies. Candy, desserts and sweets are good to avoid, and fairly easy to eliminate from our diet if we are seeking to lose weight.*

Gluttony carries the connotations of glut, gorge, satiate, excess, fill and surfeit.

TEACHING SECTION V:

Skinny Gluttons / Fat Deliverance

SKINNY GLUTTONS / FAT DELIVERANCE

The fact that some individuals can eat two to three times the amount of food as others about the same size and remain thin doesn't in any way excuse their gluttony, nor assure that they don't have a spirit. It is as much a sin as if they weighed 300 pounds. A spirit can cause someone to eat a little food or even normal amounts and still lose weight as with anorexia nervosa, or to eat much food and either lose or retain normal weight as with bulimia.

Many people with eating disorders have a problem not so much with weight, as with food. They are addicted to a particular food or type of foods, such as the "choc-o-holic" who may have no problem with other foods. Another category is composed of those who can't resist any kind of sweets, or desserts. We have dealt with people who are addicted to all kinds of food, who literally will eat anything and everything they can hold. Others, such as certain kinds of alcoholics, may become addicted to just one particular flavor or type of alcohol.

We once ministered to a man for whom we'd prayed previously who'd been delivered from alcoholism, but while living in France allowed himself to be sucked back into Satan's trap. He was lured through courtesy into going to a 'tasting' of the locally produced fine wines. He had never previously cared for wine, but he was ensnared again through Satan's subtle trick: his host pressured him to attend and taste the region's prize vintage.

We have no difficulty accepting the fact that guilt and nervousness can cause a physical condition within the body, such as ulcers. Likewise it's fairly obvious that hate, guilt, or nervousness related to shame can cause eating problems. But another less obvious, possibility is that of deep-sin guilt of another kind.

The following cases illustrate this truth. . . .

CASE 11   OLIVIA'S STORY

Inez related an amazing story in *Ministering To Abortion's Aftermath*. One part of her account has a bearing upon our present consideration. In her own words:

"A sister-Christian, Olivia, came to have me pray for her. She had the terrible disease anorexia nervosa, and wanted me to pray with her for her healing. Before we could pray, however, she suddenly looked me straight in the eyes and blurted out a statement that shocked me, 'I know why I have my anorexia nervosa, and I know why I have the terrible migraines and period problems!' (She spends four or five days a month too sick to get out of bed, Inez explained.) Olivia continued, 'It is because I HAD AN ABORTION WHEN I WAS 18!'"

"I couldn't believe that someone was actually saying those words out loud," Inez exclaimed. "I can understand your feelings because I have had one too, and so has my daughter." And then I broke down and wept right along with her. That was the first time in my life that I had ever uttered those words aloud. The words 'my abortion' had never passed my lips before."

Inez then prayed with Olivia and cast out the dual spirits of *Murder* and *Abortion,* just as she did with Nola in the following incident.

"Another friend, Nola, came one day to my home to have coffee and as we were sharing she broke down and told me how truly miserable she was. She also blurted out that she too had had an abortion. (I seem to keep running into people lately who have had abortions.) I was able to share with her some of the things you had shared with me, and especially *that the abortion was viewed by God as murder and had to be confessed to Him as murder.* Believe it or not, *I* then prayed with her and she confessed it all to the Lord, and we broke that curse of abortion and murder and misery over her and her family. She just bawled and bawled, and then God gave her a fantastic peace."

"I praise God that I am now free and also that I am able to share that freedom with others as He opens the door," Inez said as she reached for her purse and prepared to leave.

OBSERVATIONS:

(1.) Olivia recognized instinctively that the actual source of her affliction was due to the abortion. She knew that the abortion was sin, that it could open her up to, or allow disease within her body. She very clearly made the association which many have missed.

(2.) Inez having experienced deliverance herself from the aftermath of abortion, was able to help others find freedom. Being able to share the truth, helps set the captives free.

I was about to be shown another odd root source of an eating disorder through Edith. . . .

CASE 12   EDITH'S STORY: FEEDING HATE

A short, jovial heavy woman entered my prayer room. "Hello. I'm Edith," she announced. "I appreciate your seeing me on fairly short notice." Actually her niece had called a few days earlier. "I am traveling with my daughter who is the lead ballerina in the production of *Cinderella*, which is appearing in St. Louis this week, and that's how I happen to be in town."

"I have a real problem with gluttony," she stated bluntly. "I have prayed and prayed about it. The doctors have told me that I'm killing myself by carrying all this extra weight, but I just can't do anything about it."

"I've been to those 'fat farms,' have gone through several of the weight reduction programs, and never lost more than about 10 pounds, and gain it right back as soon as the program ends. As you can tell, I'm probably between one hundred and one hundred fifty pounds overweight right now."

"I have even had my church prayer group pray with me, but nothing seems to help . . . that's why I'm convinced that it is demonic and is *Gluttony*. And besides," she continued hurriedly, "I really don't eat all that much."

I learned from her that she was saved and had already been baptized in the Holy Spirit, so we proceeded with the deliverance. Edith could think of no logical reason, or spiritual cause for her weight problem. Since in our discussion I was unable to uncover any clues to the presence of any other spirits, I proceeded somewhat reluctantly to pray with her against *Gluttony*, even though I felt that if Gluttony had been her real problem, she would have gained the victory over it by this time with all the prayer that had been devoted to it.

Commanding *Gluttony* to leave didn't get much reaction, and so I commanded any related spirits that were tormenting her and causing her unnatural weight gain to manifest themselves, to name themselves, and to come out of her.

Edith began to growl in a gutteral voice, and a deeper voice suddenly boomed out, "Feeding Hate." I'd never heard of such a spirit, but nonetheless I commanded it to leave, and had her to do likewise, in Jesus' name.

She had a violent reaction: coughed, gagged profusely, and it was gone!

"I felt it go!" She exulted, but then asked me, "What is a spirit of *Feeding Hate* anyway?"

"A spirit of *Feeding Hate*," I attempted to explain as understanding was dawning upon me, "is a spirit that causes you to eat because of hatred. Apparently there's someone whom you hate and the particular nature of this spirit of hate causes you to express that hatred by feeding yourself. Who is it that you hate?"

"I guess it's my husband. Our marriage has been bad for years. I feel he has rejected me, and I guess my feeding myself is a way of getting back at him for his rejection of me. I suspect I must be eating to get even and to become even less desirable to him. That doesn't seem to make any sense, but I think it's true.''

So I had Edith forgive her husband for hurting her, rejecting her, and together we went through the steps of forgiveness. I then prayed for the healing of her body, and for the Lord to help make the unnatural weight gain come off quickly and easily.

Edith departed beaming and promised to let me know when the weight came off.

True to her word, two months later I received a letter in which Edith stated, ''I still can't believe it, but I have already lost over sixty pounds, without any dieting or any effort whatsoever on my part. The weight has just 'melted' off me.''

OBSERVATIONS:

(1.)   All natural means of dealing with her weight problem had proved unsuccessful, because the root problem was supernatural.

(2.)   An important key, not to be overlooked, was Edith's readiness for ministry. She came driven by the same ''holy desperation'' that drove the crowds out into the wilderness seeking Jesus for healing. She was ready: she didn't quibble nor seek to rationalize. When *Feeding Hate* manifested itself she readily admitted whom she hated, without seeking to excuse or justify herself. She was willing to be totally open before God.

DELIVERANCE TECHNIQUES EMPLOYED:

(1.)   Having exhausted my own knowledge and experience, and since neither Edith nor I knew what the particular root spirit was, I was forced to command the spirit involved to name itself which it had to do.

(2.)   Another thing which we usually attempt to do, is to pray for healing in areas of the body where the enemy has made inroads. In her case we prayed for a healing of her body from the effects of the weight gain.

> **REVELATION:**
> SUSPECTED GLUTTONY WASN'T THE PROBLEM.

> **REVELATION:**
> *FEEDING HATE* HAD CAUSED UNNATURAL WEIGHT GAIN.

> **REVELATION:**
> HATE TENDS TO BE SELF-DESTRUCTIVE. IT WOULD HAVE KILLED HER PREMATURELY HAD IT REMAINED UNDETECTED.

> **REVELATION:**
> WHEN THE SPIRIT WAS CAST OUT, THE WEIGHT CAME OFF.

Although this was certainly a root new to us, gluttony is most commonly rooted in either Rejection or Rebellion. . . .

CASE 13   JEANNE: GLUTTONY Rooted in REBELLION

Gluttony may be rooted in either rebellion or rejection. An example of one rooted in rebellion is Jeanne.

Jeanne was a young woman who felt rejected by her mother and so she rebelled. She explained, "My mother and I just never did get along." As a result the daughter subconsciously 'let herself go' to spite her mother, who was fastidious about her own appearance, always impeccably dressed and going to exercise classes to keep her figure trim. Jeanne, who was intelligent, college-educated, and relatively sophisticated, 'just let herself go.' Her rebellion expressed itself as a "good girl" might, by her dressing casually, almost sloppily, and by not caring about her weight. She ate indulgently as a means of *Retaliation,* a variation of the *spirit of Feeding Hate.* Subconsciously she attempted to get even with her mother, or to make a statement to her mother that the latter's life-style was wrong.

GLUTTONY Rooted in REJECTION

Gluttony may also be rooted in rejection. Some cases we've dealt with have been situations where those who were overweight had yielded to, overindulged, or rewarded themselves with food. Food can be used as a narcotic. It is used as a pain killer to offset the pain and hurt of rejection.

Eating tends to feel good, to make us feel satisfied and peaceful. The satisfying of our physical hunger sometimes lessens or offsets the hunger for affection or acceptance. The person who suffers a social setback may go on an eating binge in much the same way that an alcoholic will seek to drown his problems in alcohol. Some will eat as a result of *nervousness,* a habit rooted in *insecurity.* Some of us can readily identify with the person in an awkward social situation, such as a social function where you know no one else. How often we head directly for the appetizers. I don't think I'm alone when I realize that I'm eating more appetizers than I need. I'm eating, motivated out of nervousness, not out of real hunger.

PART SIX

Satan's Wiles

Teaching Section VI:
Negative Motivation —
Beware of Satan's Wiles

I have a friend who told me recently that he was on the new "Seafood Diet."

Being a lover of seafood, of course I 'bit' and asked, "What's the new Seafood Diet?"

*He laughed and said, "Whenever I **See** food, I eat it."*

TEACHING SECTION VI:

Negative Motivation:
Beware of Satan's Wiles

NEGATIVE MOTIVATION:
BEWARE OF SATAN'S WILES

Recognize a very basic truth: Satan hates to lose someone whom he has ensnared or taken captive. Thus, there will be a battle when you determine to be free. He will do everything within his power to prevent you from dieting, or curbing your appetite.

Satan's wiles come into play as soon as one attempts to do something about one's eating habits, or weight. If you think you've never heard Satan's voice, just listen after making the decision to diet or to control your appetite.

"You can't diet. You never have been able to. It hasn't worked for you in the past, why think it will work this time?"

"You can't diet now, because you need all your strength for the tasks you've got to perform at work. You'll get weak!"

"Let's wait on dieting till next summer when you're on vacation."

"Let's start next week, because there's that nice potluck, and ice cream social planned at church tonight."

"You can't cut down on your food intake; you'll starve. Why do you think your body has been requiring all that food? You need it!"

"You'll get sick if you don't eat."

If you make the mistake of waiting for a convenient time, you'll find like Pilate, that a convenient time never comes.

Fasting & Dieting

"I get headaches if I don't eat" is an alibi I have heard hundreds of times from people who would seek to excuse themselves for not fasting.

Observation: Fasting is not dieting, but fasting will help you to establish or regain rule over your own body, and your appetites. Expect a battle, especially when spirits are involved, or if habits are well entrenched.

To restate some of his common wiles which have already been covered:

The enemy of our souls and bodies would like to convince us that

(DECEPTION #1)   WE'RE MADE BY GOD TO BE FAT (fatalism)

(DECEPTION #2)   WE CANNOT CHANGE OUR APPETITES

(DECEPTION #3)   WE CANNOT CHANGE OUR WEIGHT

(DECEPTION #4)   WE MUST ACCEPT OURSELVES JUST AS WE ARE

These are all lies of the Enemy. He wants us to believe his lie, ''I can't change!'' It is difficult to discipline oneself, especially if you weren't taught discipline as a child. But it is still possible!

Satan would love for us to remain as we are, to believe that we cannot change, to believe that *even God* couldn't help us change, and therefore we must remain as we are . . . vulnerable to his condemnation for not changing: condemned for being overweight, and not liking our appearance, nor respecting ourselves.

A simple observation and a little logic can put the lie to Satan on all of these points: consider all those who have successfully lost weight and kept it off. They are those who aren't complaining about how diets don't work.

A new wile with which you may be hit, is of lesser significance, but also serves as a deterrent to dieting or restraint, and that is ''fat organizations,'' which are a type of natural counterpart to the Debbie Diet groups. Today there are well-intentioned organizations, which have roots in self-indulgence, self love, and rebellion, such as ''True Beauty Is Fat.'' The names may vary, but the thrust is basically the same: Love yourself, just as you are. You don't have to change. Don't let society or someone else's perception of either 'beauty' or 'normal' influence you.

The rebellious aspect in this thinking is an unwillingness to accept any standard other than that of their own will, and in their rejection of conforming. The true danger of such groups is that normally the spokesperson is at least 300 pounds and they encourage people by example, who are similarly grossly overweight to remain that way. The members are potentially deterred from losing the excess weight which puts undue strain upon the heart and other vital organs. Such groups exert only a mild motivational deterrent to those who are only slightly overweight, but they may have a life threatening effect upon those tragically overweight who take the easy route and give up on any attempt at restraint.

Some of Satan's other whipsawing lies we have already encountered . . .

"If you lose this weight the *Jezebel Spirit* will return."

"If you lose the weight you'll be a source of temptation again to men who will view you with lust." This is especially a snare for those who were raped or molested in their early years.

"What if you lose this weight and you are still a failure? What if losing the weight doesn't help your self-image or personality?"

"What if you go to all this effort and it doesn't work?"

In the following case Satan used just such bizarre rationales and added a few new wrinkles. . . .

CASE 14   MARGARET'S STORY

Margaret, a sweet Christian lady who had been saved and Baptized in the Holy Spirit in our prayer room, scheduled an appointment and came for deliverance. As she sat across from me, I noted that her weight still seemed abnormally great. She was probably somewhat over 300 pounds. As we talked, several classic overweight symptoms and syndromes came to light. Margaret rewarded herself with sweets.

"THE REWARD" SYNDROME

One may become addicted to candy or sweets as a child when rewarded by parents with candy. A common pattern we have observed is the individual who was rewarded with sweets as a child, to then carry into adulthood the practice of rewarding himself in the same manner. This is what Margaret had done.

She, like many other women whom we have encountered, rewarded herself for completing the ironing with an ice cream sundae, or a piece of pie. Then the practice spreads to include a couple of cookies for doing the dishes. A subtle aspect of this problem is that it is most often "closet-eating." No one else knows that the woman is doing it, and thus when the family is around she can eat sparingly and even appear to be dieting. This sometimes leads to the martyristic role of one who says, "I just can't seem to lose weight. You know how little I eat at meals." The deception only compounds the guilt over being a secret, or "closet-eater." This is the same guilt we noted in the case of Charity.

Margaret is an excellent illustration of several of the unnatural weight gain syndromes, which we have encountered. Although she sincerely thought that she was coming to lose *Gluttony*, her weight problem had several different roots. She initially described her particular problem as being rooted in the fact that she was truly a "choc-o-holic."

A TRUE "CHOC-O-HOLIC"

We have already touched upon addictions to foodstuffs, such as chocolate. However, Margaret did not merely eat the candies from a fancy box of chocolates, but when they were gone, retrieved the paper wrappers from the waste basket, sniffed them, licked them, and sucked on them. She was ashamed and offended by her own actions.

I could identify with her problem in a certain sense. I

almost never buy a piece of candy, but if someone were to hand me a box of chocolates, and I were to eat one of them, I could just as easily eat the whole box. Thus, I make it a matter of personal decision not to eat the first one.

Margaret's situation had the classic patterns: rewarding herself with sweets for completing household tasks, and fixation upon chocolate. Her case was unique with what I now describe as the "Camouflage" Syndrome.

THE "CAMOUFLAGE" SYNDROME

Satan will often use some bizarre thought processes to ensnare or reinforce his hold upon his victim. Even though the thought processes seem to be totally irrational and illogical to one on the outside looking in, to the victim they seem totally logical.

We determined in the pre-deliverance interview that her overweight problem, which was extreme, had begun shortly after an extra-marital affair. She had been deeply guilt-stricken over the affair and resolved mentally and apparently deeper, that it would never happen again.

She said, "You wouldn't believe it to look at me now, but I once had one of the most fantastic bodies you've ever seen. I used to make several hundred dollars a day modeling. I could have been a movie starlet. As a young woman I had a marvelous shape. I'm not exaggerating or bragging; it was really that good. But," she said ruefully, "look at me now. I'm more than one hundred and fifty pounds overweight, and I haven't been able to touch my weight by exercising or dieting . . . nothing helps."

The clue was given when she related to us when the problem had started. She had made a decision internally, subconsciously, perhaps in her heart, that she *would never again be a source of temptation to any man.* Thus she invited a spirit through a wish, a spoken statement or a prayer such as "I wish I were fat and no man would ever want to look at me." She did, in fact, when questioned, remember praying something to that effect, in almost those very words.

After her deliverance, Margaret is today working on her weight, and recently asked me for a 'really powerful Scripture' that she could use in doing battle with the enemy over her weight.

I offered her a couple, but the one which appealed to her the most was Philippians 4:13,

"I can do all things through Christ which strengtheneth me."

She said, "I'll take that one for my 'dynamite' to blast the enemy out of his trenches."

A week later she called to report, "I have lost 21 pounds, without a struggle. The Scripture," she said, "has done its job!" A listing of similar POWER SCRIPTURES will be found in the back of this book.

Another category or common weight related problem syndrome is what I have come to call the

"CONNIE, CONSTANT PRAYER CANDIDATE" SYNDROME

Frequently while holding healing services, I am made acutely aware of this category of individual. I'm sure you have seen them, too. Every time there is an opportunity for prayer "Connie the constant prayee" is always in the front of the line. I do not wish to discourage anyone from earnestly seeking and even asking more than once, because persistent prayer is often needed. However, Connie is there with a different motive. She is typical of those people whom you can find in most assemblies who are always looking for a 'quick fix,' a miracle cure, or a new minister passing through town who can wave a 'magic wand' and make their problems disappear without any effort upon their part.

Similarly, I have also seen hundreds of cases of people, especially grossly overweight women, who are always in the prayer chair for ministry, for problems with their knees, legs, hips, etc., who would have no, or certainly far less, problems with their legs if they weren't carrying so much excess weight. Many have admitted that that's exactly what the doctors have told them, when I've been bold enough to ask them bluntly.

One man who was probably more than 200 pounds overweight came for prayer in a service one evening. I asked why he needed prayer, and by way of answer, he pulled up his trouser cuffs to reveal discolored, blue legs. He explained, ''The doctors say because of my weight, my legs aren't getting enough circulation and they want to amputate them.''

A tragic case but clearly indicating that many physical problems and ailments may be due to a lack of self-discipline. If our assumptions are correct, the demonic weight problems of such people may well be the roots behind various other physical disorders.

OBSERVATIONS:

SELF-DESTRUCTIVE PRAYERS

(1.) Self-destructive prayers, like sin-motivated prayers are not in accordance with either the will or the word of God and therefore are not eligible for Him to hear or answer.

> ''And this is the confidence that we have in him, that, if we ask any thing according to his will, he heareth us:
>
> ''And if we know that he hear us, whatsoever we ask, we know that we have the petitions that we desired of him.''   (I John 5:14,15)

God, upon the basis of His own word cannot hear prayers that are unrighteous or not in accordance with His will. However, there is one who loves to hear such prayers; one who is a liar, a thief and a murderer (John 8:44), and who loves to answer prayers motivated by sin, lust or a desire for self-destruction.

Significantly since sin-motivated prayers are not, by definition, righteous nor properly hearable by God, they would seem to fall into a category similar to the prayers offered to Satan by his own followers. This is an awesome thought, and a definite encouragement to pray both carefully and righteously.

(2.) Margaret, like most grossly overweight people, had bought the enemy's lie that she was guilty of gluttony, and assumed that to be her problem.

(3.) She had tried a variety of weight reduction gimmicks, programs and systems, all to no avail. Her situation was also compounded with a broad spectrum of other deliverance needs, beyond the immediate weight problem. She had rejection problems which stemmed in part from her shape, problems stemming from relationships, contact with alcoholic relatives, and a major involvement with false religions and the occult. It took several sessions just to deal with the underlying problems.

(4.) She had fallen prey to the reward syndrome and needed to take a stand, make a decision, to resist that pattern and to change her habits, which she did.

(5.) The choco-holism deliverance was fairly easy, as she had already determined to be freed from it before she came.

(6.) The Camouflage syndrome's hold was also deftly broken, largely due to her recognition of the problem, then confession, repentance, renouncing it.

(7.) Proverbs 18:21 states that "Death and life are in the power of the tongue." What we say, and even more, *what we pray is extremely significant.* Praying is not something to be taken lightly. God is serious about prayer, and so is the devil. If Satan can get us to pray lustful, or sin-motivated prayers, he can really get his hooks into us.

> ## REVELATION:
> THE DANGER OF SIN-MOTIVATED, AND
> SELF-DESTRUCTIVE PRAYERS.

> ## REVELATION:
> THAT A SPIRIT COULD TAKE ADVANTAGE OF
> THE "CAMOUFLAGE" SYNDROME TO MAIN-
> TAIN BONDAGE.

The Lord had another teaching case for me which although tinged with humor would again confirm truths about what we'd learned of *Gluttony*. . . .

CASE 15   FAT DELIVERANCE

A few years ago I received a call from a woman in a rural community about 40 miles south of us, asking if she could come "to have a demon of *Gluttony* cast out." We set an appointment for the following week. She called again a few days later and asked if she could bring her entire prayer group for deliverance. "How many are in your prayer group and from what do they *all* need deliverance?" I asked somewhat dubiously.

She attempted to reassure me, "It's a fairly small group: there are only seven and one can't come. We all need deliverance from the same thing . . . *Gluttony*."

I warned her that my prayer room was rather small and that we might have to put some of the group on folding chairs in the hallway, but we'd manage somehow. I must confess that I didn't think we'd get them all in. I recalled the time when I had a mother and son come together for deliverance. Both weighed over 300 pounds, and we were literally wedged against the prayer room's walls. We have since remodeled and now have a larger prayer room.

I was anticipating with mixed emotions the forthcoming 'fat deliverance.' I was pleasantly shocked. Oddly enough, not one of the women who came for deliverance was what I would have described as fat. A couple were large, but none were even plump, and some were actually thin. But they had the same complaint, 'compulsive eating,' which they all considered to be a spirit of *Gluttony*.

I briefly explained to them about demons and how they operate. I also related Mary's account to them which ministered to them tremendously. There is such an anointing upon the truth contained in Mary's story that many people are set free simply by hearing it and coming to grasp its implications. I explained the whipsawing effect that the demons endeavor to maintain . . . of hitting you with a fear and then condemning you for having a fear. In their particular case, I made the application of Satan causing them, for whatever rationale to overeat, and then condemning them because they did overeat or put on weight. He is a liar and a thief and he wants to steal their joy!

Next, I bluntly told them, ''I doubt that any of you have gluttony *per se*, because you have been praying so ardently against that, you'd probably have been delivered long ago when you all prayed for one another. What you have instead is *something else* that manifests itself in over-eating, or unnatural weight gain.''

Several of the women received deliverance from other problems that seemed unrelated, but actually were related: *Rejection*, feelings of being *Unloved* or *Unwanted by Parents*, and several lost spirits of both the *Fear of Starvation* and the *Fear of Abandonment*. We finished the session by praying against every spirit of *Unnatural Weight Gain*, including *Gluttony* just to cover all the bases, and our old enemy *Feeding Hate* surfaced again, along with *Inferiority*, and were also cast out.

PART SEVEN

Epilogue

Appendices

*** WEIGHT CONTROL TIPS ***
*** POWER SCRIPTURES ***
*** INDEX OF EVIL SPIRITS ENCOUNTERED ***

Epilogue

Although many have attempted to cover up for their weight problems with levity, there is really nothing at all funny about being overweight.

We have encountered many unusual sources of over-eating in this book, but the losing of weight still boils down, as does all progress with God, to an individual decision. The ball is in your court: if you are overweight, you must make the decision to do something about it. No one else can do it for you. Your decision may be simply to acknowledge the source of your overeating and to take a stand against it; it may be a decision to eat less or to avoid certain food groups; it may even be a decision to prayerfully cast out the root spirit(s) which the Lord has revealed to you as being the source of your eating problem.

The people whose accounts you have just read, all had one thing in common: every one of them made a decision to seek help, to get prayer for their conditions. It was only as they were in motion, seeking God, that He could guide them. The greatest guidance systems in the world only function when the vehicle is in motion. As an example the huge rudder on the Queen Elizabeth II, cannot give that ship any guidance so long as the ship remains at the dock. It is only as the great ship begins to move, that the rudder can have an effect and steer her.

So it is most often with us. We only seem to receive God's guidance and direction as we begin to move, to step out in faith. Thus, I would encourage you to exercise self-control, and if you need to lose weight, use your will power; will power plus prayer; will power plus prayer plus fasting; and if indicated, will power plus prayer plus fasting plus deliverance. If you feel that deliverance is needed, I would suggest that you read Volume 1 in this series, *Songs of Deliverance* and/or some of the other books on deliverance recommended in that volume, and follow the steps indicated.

You should also seek out a counselor. It could be your pastor, a relative, a prayer partner, or some prayer warrior whom you respect and can trust. Discuss your weight problems with them and have them pray in agreement with you in your battle.

There are several benefits from having a counselor, beyond the possibility of receiving good counsel and Godly wisdom. Having a prayer partner helps you realize that you aren't battling alone, and it serves as an additional incentive to continue resisting weight gain, *because you have made a commitment before a witness to lose the weight!*

I don't pretend that losing weight will be easy, simple or quick for all (for some it will be) . . . but I do guarantee that the fruit of your victory will be sweet!

*** Weight Control Tips ***

1. AVOID if possible eating when tired.
2. AVOID if possible eating in Smorgasbords or places which serve unlimited portions (the all-you-can-eat type menus).
3. AVOID eating too fast. When one eats in a rush, he tends to eat more than he would at a more leisurely pace. The body's normal appetite control system doesn't have a chance to make you feel full.
4. AVOID listening to fast music while eating. Music with a rapid beat will often cause one to eat more rapidly and more quantity than would be the case, if one were listening to soft, relaxful music. (When you eat in a high class restaurant what type of music do they play?)
5. Try drinking a glassful of water before a meal. This tends to lessen the sensation of hunger and fills you somewhat beforehand.
6. Eat slowly — people often bypass the body's natural indicators of being full by eating too rapidly. It apparently takes about twenty minutes for the body to normally tell itself that it is full.
7. Avoid drinking alcoholic beverages, even a glass of wine before dinner. I have found this to either dull the appetite control center in the brain, or to stimulate the appetite, and as a result one finds oneself eating more than one intends or needs.

Also try experimenting with substitutes for foods that you know to be fattening. Such as:

A substitute for sour cream. . . . Place cottage cheese in blender: blend and add just enough milk to obtain the desired consistency.

*** Power Scriptures ***

Eph. 6:10 "Finally, my brethren, be strong in the Lord, and in the *power of his might.*"

Col. 3:1 "If ye then be risen with Christ, *seek those things which are above*, where Christ sitteth on the right hand of God."

1 Thess. 2:12 "That ye would *walk worthy of God*, who hath called you unto his kingdom and glory."

1 Thess. 4:3,4 "For this is the will of God, even your sanctification, that ye should abstain from fornication: That every one of you should know how to *possess his vessel in sanctification and honour.*"

1 Tim. 4:1,3 "Now the Spirit speaketh expressly, that in the latter times some shall depart from the faith, giving heed to seducing spirits, and doctrines of devils; forbidding to marry, and commanding to abstain from meats, which God hath *created to be received with thanksgiving* of them which believe and know the truth."

1 Tim. 4:15 "Meditate upon these things; give thyself wholly to them; that thy profiting may appear to all."

1 Tim. 6:6,8 "But godliness with contentment is great gain. And having food and raiment let us *be therewith content.*"

1 Tim. 6:12 *"Fight the good fight of faith."*

2 Tim. 2:3 "Thou therefore *endure hardness*, as a good soldier of Jesus Christ."

2 Tim. 4:18 "And the Lord *shall deliver me from every evil work*, and will preserve me unto his heavenly kingdom: to whom be glory for ever and ever. Amen."

Tit. 2:12 "Teaching us that, denying ungodliness and worldly lusts, *we should live soberly, righteously, and godly,* in this present world;"

James 1:2,3 "My brethren, *count it all joy* when ye fall into divers temptations; Knowing this, that the trying of your faith worketh patience."

James 4:6,7 "But he giveth more grace. Wherefore he saith, God resisteth the proud, but giveth grace unto the humble. *Submit yourselves* therefore to God. *Resist the devil, and he will flee from you.*"

James 5:16 "Confess your faults one to another, and pray one for another, that *ye may be healed.*"

1 Pet. 1:7 "That the trial of your faith, being much more precious than of gold that perisheth, though it be tried with fire, might *be found unto praise and honour and glory at the appearing of Jesus Christ:*"

1 Pet. 2:11 "Dearly beloved, I beseech you as strangers and pilgrims, *abstain from fleshly lusts,* which war against the soul;"

1 Pet. 4:2,3 "That he *no longer should live the rest of his time in the flesh* to the lusts of men, but to the will of God. For the time past of our life may suffice us to have wrought the will of the Gentiles, when we walked in lasciviousness, lusts, excess of wine, revellings, banquetings, and abominable idolatries:"

1 Pet. 5:8,9 "Be sober, be vigilant; because your adversary the devil, as a roaring lion, walketh about, seeking whom he may devour: Whom *resist stedfast in the faith, knowing that the same afflictions are accomplished in your brethren* that are in the world."

2 Pet. 2:9 "The Lord knoweth how to *deliver the godly out of temptations,* and to reserve the unjust unto the day of judgment to be punished:"

1 John 1:9 "If we confess our sins, he is faithful and just *to forgive us our sins,* and to cleanse us from all unrighteousness."

1 Cor. 10:13 "There hath no temptation taken you but such as is common to man: but God is faithful, who will *not suffer you to be tempted above that ye are able;* but will with

the temptation also *make a way to escape,* that ye may be able to bear it.''

Eph. 3:16 ''That he would grant you, according to the riches of his glory, to be *strengthened with might by his Spirit in the inner man;*''

Gal. 2:20 ''I am crucified with Christ: nevertheless I live; yet not I, *but Christ liveth in me:* and the life which I now live in the flesh I live by the faith of the Son of God, who loved me, and gave himself for me.''

Phil. 4:13 ''I *can do all things through Christ* which strengtheneth me.''

Prov. 19:15 ''Slothfulness casteth into a deep sleep; and an *idle soul shall suffer hunger.*''

Prov. 27:7 ''The full soul loatheth an honeycomb; but to the *hungry soul every bitter thing is sweet.*''

Prov. 23:2 ''And *put a knife to thy throat,* if thou be a man given to appetite.''

Prov. 15:15 ''All the days of the afflicted are evil: but he that is of *a merry heart hath a continual feast.*''

1 Cor. 10:31 ''Whether therefore ye eat, or drink, or whatsoever ye do, *do all to the glory of God.*''

1 Tim. 4:4 ''For every creature of God is good, and *nothing to be refused,* if it be received with thanksgiving.''

Luke 1:37 ''For with God *nothing shall be impossible.*''

Prov. 30:8,9 ''Remove far from me vanity and lies: give me neither poverty nor riches; *feed me with food convenient for me:* Lest I be full, and deny thee, and say, Who is the Lord? or lest I be poor, and steal, and take the name of my God in vain.''

2 Cor. 6:16a ''And what agreement hath the temple of God with idols? for *ye are the temple of the living God.*''

Mat. 19:26 ''But Jesus beheld them, and said unto them, With men this is impossible; but *with God all things are possible.*''

Mk. 9:23 ''Jesus said unto him, If thou canst believe, *all things are possible to him that believeth.*''

2 Cor. 4:17 ''For our light affliction, which is but for a

moment, worketh for us a far more exceeding and *eternal weight of glory;''*

Index of Spirits
Encountered in This Book

*** POSSIBLE ADDITIONAL RELATED SPIRITS ***

Addictions
Compulsions
Obsessions
Gluttony
Bodily illness
Fear of disapproval
Nervousness
Frustration
Idleness
Laziness
Lethargy
Slough (If any would not work, neither should he eat.
        2. Thes. 3:10)
Self-Indulgence
Self-Pity
Self-Reward
Resentment
Greed

IMPACT BOOKS, INC.

Announces

The Exciting New Power for Deliverance Series:

Power for Deliverance; Songs of Deliverance
Power for Deliverance From Fat

Lives have already been changed by the powerful truths and revelations contained in these books as the author has taught them over the past seventeen years. These deliverance tools have been tested in the crucible of prayer room battles to free lives from Satan's control. You have tasted in this book the kind of dramatic accounts and truths which are to be found in the other volumes in this series.

Each book is just $5.95. When ordering add $1.50 postage and handling for the first book and $.50 for each additional title.

Available at your local Christian bookstore, library, or directly from:

IMPACT BOOKS, INC.
137 W. Jefferson
Kirkwood, MO 63122

Powerful Help on Cassette

Are You Saved? Have You Been BORN AGAIN? Do you even know for sure what is meant by these questions?

If not, we strongly recommend that you send for the tape
HOW TO BE SAVED, or BORN AGAIN!

To receive this informative tape, which can change your life . . . just as it has for thousands of others, when they have heard the message contained on the tape and responded to it. . . .

Simply send your name and address along with $5.00 to cover all costs to:

IMPACT BOOKS, INC.
137 W. Jefferson
Kirkwood, MO 63122

NOTE: If you honestly cannot afford to pay for the tape, we will send it to you free of charge.

POWERFUL NEW BOOK
BY SAME AUTHOR . . .

This new book is unique because it offers real help for the suffering women who have already had abortions. This book is full of GOOD NEWS!

It shows how to minister to them, or may be used by the women themselves as it contains simple steps to self-ministry.

Millions of women **have had abortions:** every one of them is a potential candidate for the type of ministry presented in this book. Every minister, every counsellor, every Christian should be familiar with these truths which can set people free.

$3.95 + $1.00 Shipping/Handling

IMPACT BOOKS, INC.
137 W. Jefferson, Kirkwood, Mo. 63122

THE HEAVENS DECLARE . . .

William D. Banks

More than 250 pages!
More than 50 illustrations!

- Who named the stars and why?
- What were the original names of the stars?
- What is the secret message hidden in the stars?

The surprising, **secret message** contained in the earliest, original names of the stars, is revealed in this new book.

. The deciphering of the star names provides a fresh revelation from the heart of **the intelligence** behind creation. Ten years of research includes material from the British Museum dating prior to 2700 B.C.

A clear explanation is given showing that early man had a sophisticated knowledge of One, True God!

$6.95 + $1.00 Shipping/Handling

ALIVE AGAIN!

William D. Banks

The author, healed over twelve years ago, relates his own story. His own testimony presents a miracle or really a series of miracles — as seen through the eyes of a doubting skeptic, who himself becomes the object of the greatest miracle, because he is Alive Again!

The way this family pursues and finds divine healing as well as a great spiritual blessing provides a story that will at once bless you, refresh you, restore your faith or challenge it! You will not be the same after you have read this true account of the healing gospel of Jesus Christ, and how He is working in the world today.

The healing message contained in this book needs to be heard by every cancer patient, every seriously ill person, and by every Christian hungering for the reality of God.

More than a powerful testimony — here is teaching which can introduce you or those whom you love to healing and to a new life in the Spirit!

$3.95 + $1.00 Shipping/Handling

BEST SELLERS FROM IMPACT BOOKS

137 W. Jefferson, Kirkwood, MO. 63122

BOOKS

_____ ALIVE AGAIN	3.95
_____ A LOVE STORY	1.25
_____ DECISION TO DISCIPLESHIP	1.25
_____ GOLD FROM GOLGOTHA	1.50
_____ GREATER IS HE!	1.25
_____ GREATER WORKS SHALL YE DO	2.25
_____ HOW TO HEAR GOD SPEAK	1.50
_____ IS FAITH REQUIRED FOR YOUR MIRACLE	2.25
_____ KINGDOM LIVING	4.95

_____ MINISTERING TO THE LORD	3.50
_____ MINISTERING TO ABORTION'S AFTERMATH	3.95
_____ MIRACLE BUS TO THE SHRINE	1.75
_____ MY PERSONAL PENTECOST	1.25
_____ PIGS IN THE PARLOR	4.95
_____ THE BLOOD COVENANT	5.95
_____ TRIAL BY FIRE	3.50
_____ THE HEAVENS DECLARE	6.95

MUSIC & SONG BOOKS

_____ DELUXE GUITAR PRAISE BOOK	2.95
_____ FAVORITE HYMNS ARR. FOR CLASSICAL GUITAR	2.95
_____ FAVORITE HYMNS ARR. FOR PIANO	2.95
_____ GOSPEL BANJO	2.95
_____ GUITAR CHRISTMAS CAROLS	1.95
_____ GUITAR HYMNAL	2.95
_____ JESUS SONGS!	2.95
_____ GOSPEL GUITAR	2.95
_____ HYMNS FOR DULCIMER	4.95
_____ LITURGICAL GUITARIST	9.95
_____ ONE WAY SONGBOOK	2.95
_____ SACRED GUITARIST	2.95
_____ SACRED ORGANIST	2.95

_____ SACRED PIANIST	2.95
_____ "SIGNS SHALL FOLLOW" SONG BOOK	2.95
_____ SPIRIT FILLED SONGS	2.95
_____ CHILDREN'S GUITAR HYMNAL	1.95
_____ HYMNS FOR AUTOHARP	4.95
_____ HYMNS FOR CLASSICAL GUITAR FOSTER	4.95
_____ MORE HYMNS FOR CLASSIC GUITAR-FOSTER	4.95
_____ SONGS OF CHRISTMAS FOR AUTOHARP	2.50
_____ LITURGICAL GUITARIST (CASS.)	7.95
_____ FAMILY HYMN BOOK	6.95
_____ HYMNS FOR HARMONICA	5.95

Bill Banks.
Terminal Cancer.
48 hours to live.
Miraculously healed!

Name _____
Address _____
_____

For your convenience, you may use either MasterCard or Visa.
MasterCard No. _____
Visa No. _____
Expiration
Date _____

PIGS IN THE PARLOR

Do You Know Anyone With CANCER?
Here's Living Proof GOD HEALS!

250,000 Copies In Print ·
ARE DEMONS REAL?

Notes

Notes

FOR ADDITIONAL COPIES WRITE:

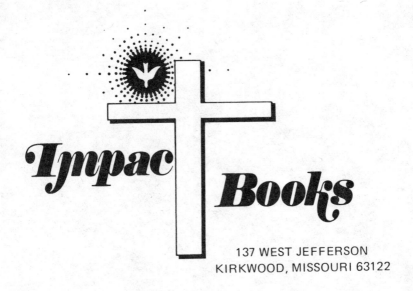

137 WEST JEFFERSON
KIRKWOOD, MISSOURI 63122